AN INDIAN LOVE AFFAIR

SIMON GANDOLFI was born in London in 1933. After military service served as a subaltern in the 16th/5th Lancers, at the age of 18, early friendships with the co-directors of the cult movie, *Performance*, introduced him to the wider world of the arts, and actor Anthony Quayle encouraged him to write his first novel, *Even With the Shutters Closed*. He has been privileged in making writing and travel his primary occupations and has been fortunate in living in and experiencing a variety of cultures: Spain/Ibiza, Greece, France, Afghanistan and the Indian subcontinent, the Dominican Republic and, finally, Cuba for four years before returning to his cottage in Herefordshire.

Arcadia Books Ltd
139 Highlever Road
London W10 6PH

www.arcadiabooks.co.uk

First published in the United Kingdom by Arcadia Books 2016
Copyright © Simon Gandolfi 2016

A catalogue record for this book is available from the British Library.

ISBN 978-1-910050-81-1

Typeset in Garamond by MacGuru Ltd

Printed and bound by T J International, Padstow PL28 8RW

ARCADIA BOOKS DISTRIBUTORS ARE AS FOLLOWS:

in the UK and elsewhere in Europe:
BookSource
50 Cambuslang Road
Cambuslang
Glasgow G32 8NB

in the USA and Canada:
Dufour Editions
PO Box 7
Chester Springs
PA 19425

in Australia/New Zealand:
NewSouth Books
University of New South Wales
Sydney NSW 2052

AN INDIAN LOVE AFFAIR

SIMON GANDOLFI

A

For my children, Antony, Mark, Anya, Joshua and Jedediah

Dear Friends,

We all hear the same sounds. We look up and see the same sky. We cry the same tears. One's feelings and emotions are the same. All mothers are sisters. All fathers are brothers. All children are one. Yet there is hatred, there is violence, there is intolerance and confusion among people. We don't try hard enough to understand each other. We don't seem to realise that we all have the same basic needs, no matter who we are and which part of the world we come from. We must understand the difference amongst us and celebrate the oneness. We must make the world a place where love and friendship dominate one's heart. Equality, respect, compassion and kindness must guide one's action; only then will we all be able to peacefully and lovingly live the life we each choose. May this year be the 'Year of Peace' for all, far and near, friends and foes.

The Principal, Loreto College, Shillong

AN INDIAN LOVE AFFAIR

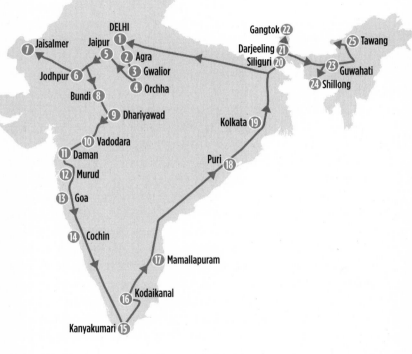

This is a journal of two explorations of the Indian subcontinent separated by 40 years, the most recent as a septuagenarian. I was 37 years old when I visited India for the first time and about to become a gold smuggler (amongst other things). I was living on the Mediterranean island of Ibiza. My travel guidebook was conversation over breakfast at a sidewalk table outside the Montesol Hotel on the town square: freshly squeezed orange juice, coffee, an *ensomada* and sunshine. I recall that David Bushman advised me to buy cheap Indian rupees. Bushman was wavy-haired, California tan with a Hasselblad camera and Rolex Oyster. *Vogue* featured his fashion-model girlfriend. He was rich. He knew about money. He presumed that other people shared his knowledge and was borderline contemptuous of those who didn't – reason enough not to ask where I should buy cheap rupees, nor why some rupees were cheap.

I had sold an apartment recently at the top of the old town. The buyer, a Belgian of doubtful probity, suggested paying the money into a Swiss bank account – a numbered account. Numbered accounts were secret and designed by Swiss bankers to hide illicit gains. The gainers were reputable financiers, master criminals, politicians, tax evaders and James Bond-type spies. Spies were romantic. The Belgian arranged my account. I was proud of it. I was moving up in the world. The sole disadvantage – I didn't know how to operate the account and was too embarrassed by my ignorance to ask.

Today's bankers run money laundries on small Caribbean islands and Central American republics. Switzerland and Lichtenstein enjoyed a monopoly in the sixties. UBS was king. My bank was small, down a side street, and built of grey stone. All Geneva was grey – except for the parks. Swiss bankers were grey and superior. They knew the world's secrets. Ask the teller whether he had cheap rupees and he replied that he would look. I imagined a vast vault protected by massive steel doors; shelves burdened with the currencies of the world sorted into neat Swiss piles: *new, clean, worn, disgusting.* Cheap would be the disgusting pile.

The teller returned. He was a young man, non-committal by nature, training, or both. Rimless spectacles, grey suit and blue-grey tie were part of it. The bank was out of cheap rupees. Why didn't I take gold?

A wiser and more confident man would have asked why. I merely looked surprised.

He said, 'It is usual to take gold.'

But how much? Nor was I certain as to how much money remained in my account. Asking would destroy the account's secrecy and probably transgress the mores of Swiss banker/client relationship. And the teller would sneer at my financial incompetence, though not visibly.

Such thoughts took a while.

The teller waited.

I pretended to calculate.

Close to one thousand eight hundred and fifty dollars suggested a calculation.

In movies, gold comes in brick-sized ingots. The teller proffered thin plaques the size of a business card.

Was I being ripped off? How to know?

'And a thousand dollars in travellers cheques,' I said…

So began my drive from Europe to India. My wheels were a canvas-top Volkswagen copy of the Wehrmacht's slab-fronted Second World War utility vehicle. Lester Waldman was my companion. A late-twenties New York Jewish photographer, Lester chronicled the alternative society. His portrait of Allen Ginsberg with the Stars and Stripes and the sun streaming out of his head was a classic.

We intended making a film of the hippy trail east. This was a joint production with TrikFilms. Lester was to photograph everything in sight. TrikFilms would project the stills on to a screen. Filming the stills with a camera that moved on rails produced the illusion of action. The producer showed us a recently edited short of a model dancing though trees in Hyde Park; David Bailey was the photographer. Lester was accustomed to shooting half a dozen rolls of 35mm for a single portrait; with TrikFilms every shot would be judged. The required accuracy of focus unnerved Lester. He also felt vulnerable in my canvas-top VW while I argued against transporting his 20-kilo sack of muesli. I hadn't mentioned the gold. Gold was dangerous; word got out and someone would whack me over the head.

Istanbul was our first way station. The area round the Blue Mosque on the European side of the Bosphorus was a hippy-inhabited mini Ibiza – Lester territory. He was reluctant to cross the bridge into Asia while I was uncomfortable amongst a homophobic Turkish community so obviously contemptuous of semi-penniless long-hairs. More rewarding was an introduction to a Russian exile resident in Istanbul for 30 years. We lunched in autumn sun at restaurants on the Bosphorus, water unpolluted in those distant days. Walk down a wooden jetty to a plank platform bearing a dozen tables: a waiter shouted our choice of fish through a megaphone to fishermen in row boats; while waiting, we snacked from a trolley loaded with a bewildering array of delicious *entremeses*.

Next came Tehran where Lester exchanged my company for a lift from a painter who shared a home with a twin brother on Ibiza's little-sister island, Formentera. I don't recall which twin; they both owned VW campers. To pay for petrol, I collected two Canadians fresh out of university and an equally young Jewish American from Chicago on the run from a career selling female underwear.

Afghanistan was dysentery and where marijuana-smoking foreigners encountered hashish for the first time. Afghani hashish was a nuclear bomb; three hits on a water pipe and the back of your head melted through the wall. Someone mentioned that carrying gold into India was a major crime. Add a female Indian Customs officer reputed to have psychic powers and I was nervous.

A baker on Kabul's Chicken Street baked chocolate brownies. The brownies came with hashish or without. *With* led to a confusing thought stream: I had driven across Europe, Turkey and Iran without thought that I was a smuggler. Gold was respectable. A Swiss banker had sold me the gold. Surely that made it legal? Blessed by a Priest of International Finance? As in taking Holy Communion. The secrets of the confessional the spiritual equivalent of a Numbered Account? God as a Tax Collector? Definitely confusing.

Better bathe my face in cold water and go easy on the chocolate brownies.

And where to hide the gold?

This far the plaques had nestled in a canvas money belt worn beneath my shirt – surely the first place a Customs officer would search.

I don't recall being concerned at entering Pakistan. We arrived at the Indian frontier with the canvas hood furled. The gold sat on the narrow shelf below the windscreen. I had rolled it in grubby toilet paper. What could be more innocent? We were fifth in a line of foreign vehicles. I recall one as a rusty orange camper painted with oms and peace symbols. Nearly an hour passed while the psychic Indian lady interrogated each driver and passenger. My gold was out in the open, unguarded, tempting to light fingers. Anxiety made me sweat. I returned to the car, picked up the gold.

A Sikh Customs officer in immaculate uniform strolled towards me.

I slipped the gold into my trouser pocket. My trousers slid to the ground. Panicked, I clutched my belly, hobbled behind the VW, yanked down my underpants and squatted beside the rear wheel. The Sikh peered down. I peered up. My face glistened with sweat. 'Dysentery,' I stuttered. 'So sorry. I do apologise.'

The Sikh spun on his heel and reported the horror to his psychic superior. She sent one of the Canadians to collect my passport, stamped us all and sent us on our way. Not a glorious entry to India but the gold was safe. Onward to Goa…

1
GOA FIRST DISCOVERED

This morning I shredded 53 pages of typed manuscript. I am trying to write a tale of two journeys and have been at the desk a month, knowing, even as I write, that the book isn't working. That the form is wrong, that I haven't captured the voice; that I am being too writerly. Doubts keep me awake at night. I am old. My mind, always untidy, doesn't work as well as it did. I forget things. The onset of Alzheimer's frightens me. I test myself each morning by attempting the *Guardian*'s concise crossword for which dyslexia is already a handicap. At home, dictionaries lurk in every room; on train journeys, I check spelling with fellow travellers. But I'm digressing, straying from the path, losing track – another accompaniment of old age, but one that I must harness to best please you, the reader.

If only I could see you…

On the lecture platform, I watch faces, am guided by expressions.

Horrors can occur, witness my most recent stay in Delhi and visiting a private high school. A teacher chivvied me upstairs to tell of my travels to a mixed class of mid-teens. A glossily groomed thirty-year-old Indian Adonis held sway as he recounted his ride on an over-engined trail bike from Colombia south to Tierra del Fuego. The Adonis was slender. He wore tailored jeans and a long-sleeve slim-fit shirt of blinding whiteness. His teeth gleamed, as did his cuff links and tasselled loafers. In command of technology, he flashed photographs. Whatever the background (mountains, cathedral, bridge or waterfall), Adonis was to the fore, his pose always nonchalant, big bike, proper biker boots and all the gear. Girl students were in full swoon mood as he recounted his adventure, dark eyes sweeping the audience. Even the boys were attentive.

I am no Adonis. These were rich kids; I rode bikes their servants rode to market. My charity shop T-shirt and cargo pants (button missing from a side pocket and frayed cuffs) failed to cut the mustard. Plus being older than their grandparents…

A few of the politest girls pretended attention. Most were exchanging Adonis fantasies; from the boys I caught scraps of cricket conversation. Not a success…

However, back to the writing difficulties. Finally, I may be getting there, the tone chatty, as in talking directly to the audience rather than giving a talk – a minimum of organisation. Of course this may be another cul-de-sac but I'll give it a go. Forget that I'm writing a book and concentrate on what you, the reader, wish to know.

I began this book with gold smuggling. Best that I continue, rather than leap from past to present and back, which must surely confuse.

As a criminal, I was a nervous neophyte. Hollywood was my tutor. In crime capers, disposal of the loot presented the major difficulty. No gold-buyers featured in my address book for India. My letters of introduction were equally barren: communist trade union leader, resident head of the CIA, a Goan architect with a Danish wife.

The immediate destination was Goa for Christmas. Of memories, few incidents remain of the journey south. India in the 1960s was different. Tourism was negligible and hotels existed solely in major cities. Only trunk roads were tar. Most travellers were government officials on inspection tours, each department of government with its inspection bungalows. The Ambassador was the official's car, painted white or pale sand, bedding rolls strapped to the roof and a chauffeur in faded khaki. A majority of trucks were military. Ox carts were the norm, always in the centre of the road, often in long trains, always overladen. Wagoners never gave way.

Lester Waldman was back with me and the American underwear salesman. (What happened to the two Canadians?) I was driving in convoy with a couple in a VW camper; Elizabette was French, he was Swiss-Italian. I don't recall where we met. They carried an Orissa wedding tent and poles on the roof rack. Lester and the bra salesman slept under the tent. I preferred the shade of a tree and carried a foam-rubber mattress sandwiched between Afghan kilims – coarse camel hair rather than wool and dyed in stripes and zigzags of earth colours. Leather straps bound the bedroll athwart the VW behind the rear seat.

We drove from the Pakistan-India border south through Rajasthan. What television has made commonplace was a revelation in the 1960s; palace followed palace, most expropriated from local rulers by Mrs Gandhi's decree and abandoned to decay. Once home to tyrants, a miasma of fear protected the palaces from vandalism and invasion by the local peasantry. We wandered alone through magical court-yards, up marble staircases that could parade 20 men abreast, brushed with fingertips marble screens of almost unimaginable delicacy.

Our campsite of gaudy wedding tent, kilims and bright blue camper was visible for miles, yet no one approached. Perhaps memories of the British Raj, so recently departed, was our protection. No need here for the barrier of thorn that shielded the campsites of my youthful service with Locust Control in Somalia, the Ogaden desert and the Northern Frontier District of Kenya. A Land Rover was my vehicle in Africa and I drove, as in India, with the canvas top furled and thus exposed to the land and its inhabitants. In Rajasthan, mem-ories of that younger Simon were my companions as I lay at night and gazed up through the branches at the stars and relished the scents of sun-powdered earth, wood smoke, dried goat and camel dung. Such was the perfume of my African youth, of my first adventures.

I have little idea of what route we took through Rajasthan. With so much to see and experience, we travelled slowly, one day manag-ing only 25 kilometres. Udaipur is the single name that sticks. We rowed to the Lake Palace, ordered tea on a terrace with views across the water to the vast palaces of the Maharajah. Decor was a delight of decadent decay, service haphazard. Now rescued by the Taj Hotel Group, luxury has replaced romance.

Slim memories remain of our passage south from Rajasthan, no recollection of passing through Bombay. I know that we hurried.

And I recall the transformation from dry heat and brittle vegetation to the lush greenery of the coast, of riverbanks guarded by giant trees, emerald rice paddy, the scrape of palm fronds, air humid and thickly scented with fish and coconut oil.

Goa's Calangute, in those days, was a dirt-street village boasting a tin-roof post office with a verandah where skinny young foreigners with long hair waited for money from Mother. The beach was further down a sand track. Coconut plantations fringed the half-mile crescent of pale gold strand. Midway was fisherman territory with a few wooden boats pulled up during the day. Old men sat in the boats' shade and mended nets while kids and women spread small fish to dry on the sand.

Beyond the boats, a few shacks edged the sand. The shacks, originally built to store fishermen's gear, were rented to Western kids at a few dollars a month and I recall a primitive restaurant beyond the shacks that served coconut rice with fish that had failed to sell in the market; taste the fish and you knew why...

Wispy casuarina pines shaded the track end of the beach. Blind George had rented a small bungalow amongst the pines as a base for an ever-changing mix of Ibiza expat society. Originally from California, Blind George was a good friend and wonderful companion. A disease in his late twenties had left him with 10 per cent peripheral vision. Travel with him and you became his eyes; hard work but rewarding in that you learned to see. I recall our visiting the Gaudí-designed gardens in Barcelona. The stone pillars in the colonnade slope inwards. Imagine an earthquake and the instant before the pillars collapse. 'Great image,' said George. 'Yeah, thanks...'

George is dead now. He misjudged the distance and stepped backwards off the flat roof of his house in San Miguel de Allende, Mexico. He was planning a rooftop extension and had been counting bricks delivered earlier that day. Sad farewell to a good friend...

As to Calangute...

Fifty or so Westerners were staying on the beach, a few more up the coast on Baga. The bungalow George had rented had a front verandah overlooking the sea and comprised a central living room and two bedrooms. Floors were clay tile; bathroom had a clay bowl with ewer and a brick bath filled by bucket from a brackish well; kitchen came with a single-burner kerosene stove; lean-to storeroom. The lavatory was a raised sentry box out back boasting a wooden bench with a hole above a concrete slab open to the rear. Do your morning duty and pigs came snuffling below – not the most comforting of experiences.

Of the two other bungalows amongst the trees, the closest was a rental to a young American couple. She was dark, New York Jewish, had the money, and preached brown rice vegetarian macrobiotics while crumbling Nepalese gold and tobacco into triple Rizlas. He was a slender long-haired blond with spiritual pretensions gained reading a kiddies' catechism of the Hindu Vedas. She had him meditate in the full lotus outdoors most evenings – sort of fashion statement, maximum visibility. Pass by and you were in danger of a dietary lecture. No, thank you…

A French Buddhist and friends occupied the third bungalow. The Frenchman, Giles, was truly spiritual. He was putting together a dope deal into New York to fund building a hermitage in Nepal for his teacher (the seventh or twenty-seventh reincarnation of a lama whose name I don't recall). Giles had bought a bulbous antique ceramic vase some four feet high. The vase was a good buy; Giles' brother-in-law was an antique dealer and knew the US market. The vase was to be packed in a slatted crate. The slats were a couple of inches apart so that Customs could see the vase. The hashish was in the slats. Hollowing the slats and pressing the hashish wafer-thin was a time-consuming work of spiritual love. Giles drove a hired truck to the New York Customs warehouse. A forklift brought the vase. One of the slats had snapped; a thin slab of hashish in clingfilm projected into the crate. Giles put his faith in the Buddha and waited for a Customs officer. The Customs officer checked the documentation, barely glanced at the crate and waved to the forklift operator to load the crate into the truck. Giles built the hermitage. There is no moral to this tale. I am relating what happened rather than advocating doing a dope deal – whatever the reason. And I have strayed once more. Forgive me. Back to the gold…

I was sitting on the verandah one Saturday morning reading an article on Goa in a previous week's *Times of India*. The article was one of a series accusing the police of ignoring sex and drug orgies on Calangute. Orgies? Where?

A quick puff might lead to an orgy. But stoned? Totally stoned? I don't think so. And stoned was the Westerner's daily beach occupation, the only abstainers those suffering from dysentery or hepatitis. I remember looking up from my newspaper that Saturday. The beach was normal for mid-morning. Sky was blue and cloudless, the sea blue without a ripple. An elderly fisherman gutted fish in the shallows, an entwined Western couple were a little further out and two Westerners were working at skin cancer. Nearest was Swedish Marie. Marie had made the cover of *Vogue* a dozen times before ageing and taking to heroin – or taking to heroin and ageing? She would shoot up for breakfast, stroll down the beach in a minimalist bikini and spread her towel where the women laid out the fish to dry. The women were accustomed to Marie and spread the fish with Marie out cold as the centrepiece.

I recall musing that the fish were Marie's protection against being accosted. It was about this time that Mapsa's chief of police drove up. He was a small friendly gentleman, somewhat plump. He had come to arrest Caroline for being naked on the beach.

Caroline was always naked on the beach. She was the Westerner sunning herself in the distance beyond the boats. A Rubenesque English twenty-something, she was a product of one of those prestigious English single-sex boarding schools that teach social superiority and viciously dangerous field games. Add a father who was an admiral or a general or air marshal and you have the picture. The closest I'd come to a relationship with Caroline was to give her a lift a few times into Mapsa. No matter how many fellow passengers, Caroline sat up front.

Arresting Caroline was an act of courage.

Saturday morning and the magistrate had agreed to try Caroline in his office. The chief of police wanted me to accompany him to pay the fine; me because I was the only foreigner on the beach with a car so people presumed that I had money. I had given what cash I had that morning to the girl who cleaned the bungalow. Banks were closed Saturdays and cashing traveller's cheques elsewhere was illegal.

The chief of police countered that the gold smuggler in Mapsa market changed traveller's cheques.

The chief of police sat up front with his driver in the police truck. A sullen Caroline had dropped a thin one-piece cotton dress over her head and sat between two constables in the back. I followed in the VW.

Sixties Mapsa was a small sleepy market town. The market was a hollow square of mostly open-fronted mini shops shaded by a tin-roof verandah. I don't recall it being particularly busy that day; Mapsa was seldom busy; excitement was driving in of an evening for a mango lassi at a fruit stand.

The chief of police stopped on the north side of the market and pointed me to one of the few closed doors. I knocked and the shop-keeper shouted at me to enter. He was middle-aged, of middle height and unremarkable features and sat behind a narrow counter the left side of the small space. With the door open, he could see the police truck. He wasn't surprised or nervous and, yes, he did cash traveller's cheques, though Saturday was a bad day; the money markets were closed. Better that I return on Monday.

I explained my immediate need to pay Caroline's fine.

The gold smuggler pondered briefly before announcing that he would pay the fine. I could repay him on Monday when I came to cash my traveller's cheques. Thus there were four of us in the waiting room outside the magistrate's office: me, the chief of police, the gold smuggler and Caroline. We men hadn't considered Caroline, that she might take her arrest personally. Worse, an affront. Her mood had shifted from depressed sullen to sullen monosyllabic hatred of the male species.

The ancient ceiling fan slapped the air overhead, whack, whack, whack. The door to the magistrate's office was ajar, gleaming floorboards and dark panelling. The chief of police took Caroline by the elbow to steer her into the august presence. Caroline slapped his hand away. No way would she plead guilty. Show her the law that forbade her being naked on the beach.

The chief of police pleaded with her to be reasonable.

Reasonable and Caroline was the wrong tack.

Casting her as Lady Bountiful was the only approach; bring her to consider the chief of police as a charity case. He had a wife and children (probably dozens). The press was hounding him. Arrest someone or lose his job. Disgrace. Probably suicide.

'Oh, all right,' said Caroline.

An upward tilt of her head and she led the chief of police into the magistrate's office.

Monday I waited for the siesta hour before visiting the gold smuggler. The door was open. He emerged from behind the curtain at the rear of the shop and switched on a wall fan. A small boy brought frighteningly sweet milk tea. The gold smuggler made a couple of telephone calls. Quick fingers on an adding machine produced an offer for my traveller's cheque some 28 per cent above the legal exchange rate. The gold smuggler counted out rupees and deducted Caroline's infinitesimal fine.

He seemed a pleasant man, harmless. Certainly not a gangster. His chinos and shirt were too lightweight to disguise a pistol.

I folded the rupees into the waterproof pouch tucked down the front of my pants. I remember my mouth being dry.

'I was wondering,' I began between sips of tea. 'The chief of police called you the gold smuggler?'

Because he was the gold smuggler, said the gold smuggler.

Yes, quite.

Despite the fan, the heat in the small shop was oppressive. Flies circled my tea.

The gold smuggler fiddled with a small transistor radio. Bollywood pop satisfied him. He leant forward a little to ask whether I had gold for sale.

I was about to pry into my money belt.

'Come,' he said and vanished behind a curtain at the back of the shop. The office was even smaller than the front shop, desk a fortification behind which the gold smuggler sat in an upright chair with his back to an antique safe. A second chair faced the desk.

I laid a single ingot on the desk.

The gold smuggler fingered it briefly, noted the hallmark of three crossed keys. 'Union Bank of Switzerland. Very good.' He didn't weigh it. Nor did he consult his adding machine. The sum of rupees he offered was incomprehensible. 'Is that being satisfactory, Mister Simon?'

He could as well have been speaking Inuit or Basque, the most basic math impossible – even adding two and two. The scratchy clicks of the safe's dial reminded me of a beetle. I watched mesmerised as the gold smuggler counted the bills. I tried cramming them into my money pouch. The pouch was too small. I rose clumsily, stuffed half into my trouser pockets, stumbled on the chair leg.

The gold smuggler said, 'Mister Simon, there is no requirement for hurry. I am not murdering you.'

'It's the math,' I said – further betrayal of those black-cowled Benedictine monks who had striven to educate me at boarding school. Logarithms, calculus, all wasted.

The gold smuggler produced a hand calculator, tapped in the Geneva market price for gold, converted to rupees. I was more than doubling my original stake.

I upped my shirt, undid my belt and laid the remaining three ingots on the desk.

The gold smuggler thought briefly before asking my travel plans, how many months I intended staying in India? Carrying so much cash was unwise. The price of gold was rising. Why didn't he keep the gold for me, converting it as and when I required rupees? He had associates throughout the subcontinent. I had only to telephone or telegraph for an address.

Why did I trust him?

Because trusting people is pleasurable.

And perhaps because not trusting him would have been embarrassing.

I was to discover, over the next three years, that his tentacles spread north across borders to Nepal and into Pakistan and on over the Khyber Pass to Kabul, Kandahar and Mazar-i-Sharif – a private bank with no closing hours. And the subcontinent offered a cornucopia of travel; cross borders north to the Hindu Kush and back to attend a festival in the foothills of the Himalayas, another the following month at India's southern tip. Goa was my base, where I celebrated my thirty-seventh birthday, and where I met my future travelling companion, Vanessa. She came walking up the beach, sarong tied above her breasts, sandals dangling from one hand. Her father was bursar at one of England's more prestigious private schools. She had graduated from university the previous year with a first in sociology, India as her specialisation. My invitation to a fresh lime was accepted with a shy smile. Whoever had been to the fridge had forgotten to replace the ice tray. We drove into Mapsa for a mango lassi. So began our relationship – such a cowardly manner of referring to something of such value.

A further 40 years would elapse before I visited India again. Goa was very different and I was no longer addicted to peace and love, hash cookies or psychedelics. A motorcycle had replaced the VW. I was writing a travel column and terrorists had attacked the Taj. Not the Taj Mahal but the hotel in Mumbai that, for a century, had played host to the rich and famous … and had become my haven in those first years of exploring the subcontinent; not because I was either rich or famous but through friendship with a kindly member of the family that owned the hotel. Now was my chance to repay that hospitality with positive publicity. Fear of terrorism had killed dead the upper end of India's tourism. Yet how dangerous could India be if an ancient Brit could tour the subcontinent on a small motorcycle?

2

RETURN TO INDIA

December of 2009, and I am back in India after 40 years. I have become respectable (somewhat) and both a writer of fiction and a travel writer. My intention is to celebrate my seventy-eighth birthday in Goa while exploring the subcontinent by small motorcycle. Half-past two in the morning and I am being driven into Delhi from the international airport in an Ambassador motorcar. The driver swerves through a gap in the dividing strip to overtake a bent-chassis truck without tail lights. We are about to smash into three headlights. This is India: three headlights are at least two trucks, possibly four.

Our car slews to the right; front tyres hit and kick over the kerb; the engine stalls. The driver is a small pigeon-chested man with short spikes of grey hair. He turns to give me a smile that displays a few black teeth, gums rotted by beetle nut.

'Bad drivers,' he says.

'Very bad,' I agree.

I open both offside passenger doors, stand between them facing away from the car and irrigate the dirt. Winter and thin trails of cigarette smoke drift from a clutch of skeletal men in dhotis crouched round a charcoal brazier outside a row of mud-and-tin shacks. Back from the highway, clumps of apartment and office buildings gleam under security lamps. A white cow with protruding hipbones sprawls on the dirt; a goat in a wool jacket chews a plastic bottle. Scents are exhaust fumes, powdered soil, charcoal, urine, spices, burning rubber, burning dung.

I zip up and get back in the car. We reverse on to the highway and continue against the traffic to the next intersection. The driver's forearm remains glued to the klaxon as he bulls his way through weaving thickets of three-wheelers stacked high with vegetables. Finally Delhi: a dirt lane crosses the Grand Bazaar to the Jyoti Mahal Hotel, firm mattress on a four-poster, shower with unlimited hot water and a flush that flushes – bliss. A good night's sleep, then breakfast…

The Jyoti Mahal Hotel is listed in my *Footprint* guide. Rajasthan kitsch is the decor. I climb the staircase to a roof terrace restaurant resplendent with multi-coloured tent tops, deep couches. The only other guest is South African, a documentary film-maker (so she tells me) from Johannesburg. Chilly December and incense rises from a couple of charcoal braziers. Coffee is weak and moderately vile. Grey smog lies over the city and saps my enthusiasm – or more accurately, saps my courage.

Will I be able to cope?

As if there are options. I am here. Get on with it.

First task is to acquire a mobile phone; I lose things, so the cheapest.

Attempting to shop on the Grand Bazaar is a mistake: back home in our small English country village five people in the pub is a crowd; nature is grey skies and multiple shades of green; a single yellow daffodil is a colour scream; a sonic boom is the slow train to Ledbury mumbling to itself as it passes under the road bridge and danger is the leg-break bowler with the visiting cricket team from Brockhampton.

So, no, I am not prepared for the mass of humanity, intensity of colours, scents and hubbub – being jostled and cursed and under constant attack by motor rickshaws and handcarts, the spitting and squeezed-nostrils nose-blowing. The mobile store is a spiritual retreat. Mobile bought, the young salesman offers me a lift to the main road on his motorcycle. Politeness makes me accept – less than a hundred yards and we suffer 10 near-death experiences; the smog makes me cough. Not yet midday and I've had enough. Back to the

Jyoti Mahal and shiver under the bedclothes – this is the quaking coward hidden from any admirers of my adventures.

A hot shower brings cheer. Safety lies in recollections. One is of a restaurant in the borderland of squatter shacks that lay between Old and New Delhi. The restaurant served a partridge in a sauce that would have placated a viciously angry and punitive God. On that first visit, a young and pleasantly plump Californian couple occupied the adjoining table. The wife bewailed having no dope to smoke: the munchies and she could have eaten more. Her husband was a scientist on a US government grant to research the evil effects of marijuana and was in Delhi to consult with an Indian recognised as the world expert. I visited their hotel the following afternoon with a small piece of hashish a friend had brought from Nepal. The gift transported the couple to a land of dreams. They were expecting the Indian scientist for tea. I have wondered often whether the scientist was impressed at finding them comatose. Ah, well…

Now, 40 years later, I take a rickshaw to the same restaurant. Concrete high-rise had devoured the shacks in the borderland between Old and New Delhi, the rickshaw driver is moderately drunk and overexposure to the tourist market has ruined the restaurant, no partridge on the menu. The drunken rickshaw driver lurks outside and stops on the return journey for a small bottle of 999 Rapidsmash whisky at a bottle shop. He shows me the label. I may have misremembered the name.

Lack of a common language has me scared. And that I have contracted bronchitis with the first inhalation of what, in Delhi, passes for air. Lack of language seems most catastrophic. Who should I talk to? Only the better-educated? Those whose parents can afford the fees at a private school? Or my fellow foreigners? Then why travel?

Best conduct myself as I would in Hispanic America. Get out on the street…

It is a narrow street of down-market apartment buildings and down-market hotels. The street was tarred some years ago by the municipality. The tar has mostly gone. I am one of a group of four men, my vantage point a plastic chair outside a tailor's shop. Of my companions, one is a travel agent, good-looking, mid-thirties, one earring. A second, Nepalese, has lived in Delhi eighteen years and works as a packer for Sikh brothers in the export business. I learn nothing of the third. He may be the tailor's brother.

The street is hosting a wedding.

The arrangers of the wedding have erected a marquee in the street. The frame of iron reinforcing rod is covered by thin washed-out saffron cotton that began life cheap and hasn't improved. Twin gates are open my end of the marquee to receive the wedding party. The gates are draped with marginally less-faded saffron. A skeletal ancient squats in the dust and weaves bouquets. A younger man wires the bouquets to the gates.

The Nepalese dismisses the flowers as cheap plastic. The wedding is for a sweeper family. 'Bad people, they will get drunk and fight. Who would rent such people a hall?'

I ask whether a permit is required to close the street.

Why would they require a permit? The occasional cow strolls the street, sheep, sometimes a goat. Why not a wedding?

Chairs, tables and a sort of altar arrive on three handcarts.

A five-man cornet and drum band herald the groom. The bandsmen wear white uniforms with red-and-gold cockaded hats. The groom, also in white, and with plastic gold threaded through his wedding turban, rides a starved white horse. Four men, not in uniform, carry an electric candelabra powered by a small generator on a push cart. Male guests or family in ill-fitting dark suits shout contradictory instructions. More speed is required in the decision-making or the horse will collapse under the groom's weight.

This is the bride's big day. The owners of a hotel beside the wedding tent give her shelter in the lobby where she cowers on a sofa surrounded by mother and aunts and siblings. She is tiny, skeletal, vulnerable and looks to be 14 at most. Which is her greatest fear? Her future husband? Or damaging the scarlet-and-gold sari and head scarf or losing a piece of the gilt wedding jewellery, all hired for the occasion?

The mother and aunts depart to add their screeches to the cacophony of shouted instructions at the marquee. Trumpets blare Indian circus music. The white horse sways. A bulging German tourist in her mid-fifties photographs the bride. Wanting close-ups of the make-up and jewellery, the German holds the camera half a metre from the child's face. The child bride remains immobile, a fear-frozen statuette. Oh that she be brought to life. Give her the courage to spit in the German lady's eye and kick her future husband in the testes...

Three days in Delhi and my confidence is seeping back. My guidebook suggests a walking tour from the Broadway Hotel at 250 rupees including lunch. The tour no longer exists. Management at the hotel telephones a guide: 2,400 rupees, no mention of lunch. I walk without a guide.

Studying a city map, advice comes from all sides. Some advice is accurate; much is incomprehensible; all is well meaning and I am rediscovering India's rhythm. Differences exist. In the sixties only naked sadhus talked to themselves. Now everyone is at it, rich and poor, men, women, children, all yacking into their mobile phones. My own mobile has enabled me to call the Honda factory 20 kilometres south of Delhi; a bike awaits. Required is the courage to collect it. A seat outside a café on a main drag is perfect for cogitation. Buildings are run-down or have never come up. The hoarding on a bookshop proclaims: ALL TYPES OF RARE PERSIAN AND URDU BOOKS. Another advertises ELECTRIC CREMATORIUM. Four laden camels plod by. Tuktuks weave between overladen trucks and buses. Rich men in cars presume on their right of way. Klaxons are obligatory and smog is horrendous.

How to ride in this bedlam?

Will bravery grow with spiritual sustenance?

A maze of alleys separates the shrine of the Sufi saint from Mathura

Road. I am amongst small men dressed uniformly in white skull-caps, long white shirts and loose white trousers. The current of worshippers draws me down narrow whitewashed alleys punctuated with small stores towards voices raised in prayer. The flow is tranquil and familiar from a dozen cities that I've travelled, cities in a dozen countries. Yet in my memory there surfaces one incident from the distant past, of crossing the frontier from India into Pakistan. The bus was crowded and I stood beside a man dressed similarly to the men I now follow to the Sufi shrine. The man was serious in himself, tall and slim, pale-eyed and with clipped grey beard. Wise might be a better description but different from that which I had felt then on the bus. He questioned me politely as to where I was going.

'Afghanistan,' I said.

Afghanistan was not a good place for me, he said. His village was a community of Sufis; I was welcome to be their guest.

He was offering more.

He was offering a retreat and a new direction.

I was certain of this and certain that I should go with him; that doing so would change my life and give me at least the chance to be a better person.

I knew all this while I said to him that friends waited in Afghanistan.

He made no attempt to persuade me.

Now, 40 years later, a guardian at the shrine beckons me to sit. His features and expression are similar to the man on the bus; gravitas fits best. We sit in silence for a while, he waiting. The river of devotees flows round us, each with his garland of flowers to further decorate the saint's tomb beneath its marble canopy. Faces are gentled by a faith so distant from the ferocity of the fanatic; comfort lies in their murmured prayers.

'I've made so many mistakes,' I say.

The guardian acknowledges my confession with a minute dip of his head. 'Yes, we all make mistakes.'

Not yet dawn and I have been awake an hour. I click the TV to BBC World News. The Iraq government is auctioning Iraq's oil fields to foreign oil companies. In getting out of bed I dislodge the water bottle on my bedside table. The top is loose. Water jets into my shoes. I wonder how many tens of thousands of people in the developing world are dependent on the bottled water industry for subsistence. For such families, clean water on tap would be a financial disaster.

I am aware, of course, that dirty water is a major cause of infant mortality.

I am aware also that my shoes are wet.

And that the US/British invasion of Iraq was more malignant than a chest infection. And that I am due to accompany a fellow guest at the Jyoti Mahal on a tour of a rescue project for street children, Salaam Baalak. The guest is the documentary film-maker from Johannesburg. Mid-thirties, she is part Indian, part Boer. She and I have breakfasted together the past four days, shared a few beers of an evening. She describes her life in Johannesburg, of the ever-present threat of violent crime, of close friends she meets each week for drinks and dinner, women resident in the comparative safety offered by gated housing. Each has suffered at least one mugging and she speaks of her anxiety on returning home as she waits for her friends to report their own safe homecoming. Now stress has defeated her. She has applied for a visa to the US, better a short-order waitress in California than a successful film-maker in Johannesburg. How sad…

We are a party of six on the tour of the rescue project. The others are Indian university students. One, a woman, is studying philosophy. Her mother is a teacher, her grandmother a school principal; she has inherited a joy in thinking. The other three students are studying for degrees that will lead to careers in the Social Services; the poor are the road to the career.

The start point of our tour is a small concrete hut the far end of the longest platform at Delhi's Central Railway Station. A dozen children well short of their teens sit on benches at a plastic table. Two good women are attempting to teach them to read and write. The children giggle when I introduce myself. Meanwhile the South African is filming two urchins on the railway platform. The urchins are movie buffs. They understand film. Hands in pockets, they swagger and smile for the camera. And they dream of becoming movie stars. Every slum child dreams. Such is the influence of Bollywood. Without such dreams there would be less disappointment, less heartbreak.

Where the platform ends, tiny shacks begin, homes to adult outcasts and their families, no running water, no sewage. I have seen worse in South America. I wrote in Peru of puzzlement as to what the *poderosos* of the country – the powerful – thought as they drove past slum encampments. I remember one such camp out in the desert. Huts were black plastic sheeting beside an illegal refuse dump. A truck had dumped a load shortly before my arrival. Men and women and children hunted through the putrid refuse. Vultures perched on the skeleton of an overturned trailer and waited their turn. Cacti held their arms aloft in surrender to the horror – or in an appeal to God.

So, no, I am not shocked at what we are shown by our guide/lecturer, himself a former street child who delights in lecturing the university students with statistics. He leads us down a potter's alley to the Salaam Baalak offices. An elderly potter turns tiny bowls in the alley – bowls to serve salt or ground pepper at the table. The potter works with a large tower of clay on the wheel, turning rapidly bowl after tiny bowl, cutting each free with a thread, setting it to dry beside its brethren. Eighteen seconds – no pause, not even as he glances up to present me with a brief smile...

Our guide asks if I wish to rest midway as we climb four flights of stairs to the charity's office. The climb is easy – I am in training after daily visits to the gym, sauna and steam room back home at Malvern Spa.

The university students take notes as our guide recounts names of street kids who had made good through being rescued. I peak into a classroom. Thirty or more children sit cross-legged on the floor. Why are they here? Why did they run from home? Hunger? Abuse? Or chasing a Bollywood dream of the kid made good? Only to find more abuse, often sexual, and narcotics (Tipex the drug of choice, cheaper than glue). From this deadly spiral Salaam Baalak strives to save them with security, education and, most importantly, the knowledge that someone cares – that these children matter, that they are of value.

They strike me as cute kids, 10 years old or 12. There is always a voice, the class comic, class leader. This one sits in the front row. Good kid, very bright. Given a chance, he will transform himself from urchin to gangster or plutocrat – or spokesperson for a splendidly corrupt politician (of which India has many).

Were this Hispanic America I would sit on the floor with them. We would talk, laugh together and perhaps learn from each other. Certainly there would be a sharing of emotions. Here the most that we can accomplish is a grin and giggle. A grin seems insufficient when confronted by 30 10-year-old former Tipex addicts. Or should that be Tipex addicts in recovery?

Chivvied into a boardroom, we sit three each side of a long table. The project manager, a glossy blond young woman from North Carolina, sits at the head of the table. She served as a volunteer with Salaam Baalak whilst studying for her sociology degree. This stint is her Masters – to be followed by a Ph.D. and thence via NGOs to a career in the State Department.

She is eloquent and professional in presenting the charity's spiel. The spiel would satisfy the *Guardian* newspaper's readership: that the street children are the victims of multinationals who have expropriated their families' land without compensation. The social sciences students scribble notes. Aged cynic, I wonder whether tending the poor and needy of India is more romantic than tending those of the United States – even socially more acceptable? Akin to driving a foreign sports car? Yet the Salaam Baalak Trust is a worthy cause. Contributions would be well spent, clothes, money, whatever. You will find them on the internet…

Afternoon and I am sipping Assam tea with the motherly manageress of a large state emporium in central Delhi. The manageress is expensively plump, beautifully coiffed, charmingly dressed and must be in her early fifties. Her husband is an engineer and their two children are professionals. I mention the street children.

'Very clever, those children,' she warns. 'Yes, very clever. But nothing can be done with them. Such people do not like to work.'

The children connect in her mind with a new servant girl. The servant girl is one of 14 children, the father a manual worker. 'We are giving her soap. Now she is wanting shampoo. Can you imagine? Shampoo! This is what these people are spending money on.'

Yes, well…

A week of humid windless winter days, of visiting historic ruins, temples, mosques, fortresses, museums and art galleries of Mughal splendour and Victorian pomposity shrouded in veils of blue exhaust fumes – anything to delay the inevitable. Finally I do it. I visit the Honda factory outside Delhi. A young PR honcho supplies charm and lunch in the canteen, introduces me to engineers, to those in design, marketing and production. I am made to feel important, my age a wonder, my venture courageous. And I am introduced to my bike.

The bike stands in the centre of a corner showroom. And what a bike – a slick 125 cc café racer designed to tempt teenagers. The showroom's glass walls gleam. The floor gleams. The bike gleams. An acolyte in white overalls caresses the fuel tank with a yellow cloth. Dust would be sacrilegious.

The bike has style – though no style could survive the addition of a big-bellied ancient Brit in the saddle. My son, Joshua, warns that there is no point in writing this account of my travels unless I tell the truth so, yes, a frightened Brit. I haven't ridden a bike since completing the 11-month ride from Tierra del Fuego to my daughter's horse farm in upstate New York. A truck hit me the first day of that ride. Whack…

An orthopaedic surgeon set my leg in the kitchen at the Hotel Argentina, Rio Grande. Bikers are a community. Messages of support and sympathy came from everywhere. Javier at Dakar Motos in Buenos Aires rebuilt the rear of the bike at nominal cost and added a cup to hold crutches. Rebuilding my confidence took longer. I lost all control once on an urban thruway in Venezuela, the road slicked with rain and vast trailer trucks loaded with pipe for the oil fields swerving lanes. Safety lay behind the locked door of a service station restroom. I sat there a while, tears, shaking. Someone knocked a couple of times, asked if I was OK. A kind man in a RV led me out of town and I was fine the rest of the ride to New York, nervous sometimes, but under control.

Now, in the factory showroom, the PR honcho and a marketeer are my audience as a maintenance engineer lists the controls. Five gears and fuel injection promise 64 kilometres to the litre and, what joy, electric start. No more endless kicking and endless sweat. Press the button, *brmmm.*

I sit astride, hands on the controls. Tiny flutters of fear return, of making a fool of myself in front of these representatives of Honda's middle management, of dropping the bike in the factory's parking lot. I imagine the highway back to Delhi. I'm not ready.

Memories come of riding for the first time after the crash. Dakar Motos is in a quiet Buenos Aires residential suburb. Lunchtime and the streets were empty. I managed half a dozen blocks at snail pace before returning to the workshop. Fourteen kilometres of thruway separated the workshop from my city-centre hotel. Javier's wife, Sandra, watched as I dismounted.

'There's less traffic at the weekend,' Sandra said.

Is my fear visible now? And I need a helmet, side panniers.

The factory will be closed Sunday. But Saturday?

Yes, the factory is open Saturday. The bike will be ready with its paperwork.

Saturday morning and the PR honcho supplies me with a silver helmet emblazoned with HONDA. HONDA similarly embellishes the back of a sleeveless jacket in thick blue denim. A photographer clicks away as I wobble a few timid circuits of the factory's parking lot. My progress is further immortalised on half a dozen mobile phones, pics to amuse middle management's offspring: *Look at the fat old clown!* A wheezing clown suffering from bronchitis. The driver of the hire car who has brought me to the factory will lead me back to the hotel. 'Slow,' I order him for the umpteenth time.

Toll gates on India's highways have a bypass for bikes. I mislay the driver at the first gate. Maybe he decided to take a different road rather than pay. The traffic is thinner than I feared and I don't panic. Road signs lead to the city centre and Connaught Circus, then towards the railway station and a left on to the Grand Bazaar and the Jyoti Mahal. The hotel staff are pleasantly impressed...

3

SOUTH TO AGRA, GWALIOR AND ORCHHA

The distance south from Delhi to Agra is a mere 245 kilometres across a land of flat dusty fields. I am packed and in the saddle by 5 a.m. The ride should be easy. It isn't. The traffic freaks me. The turnpike is six lanes with a central reservation and flyovers through towns. Half the flyovers are incomplete, bikes and vehicles funnelled into one narrow track of broken asphalt, deep ruts and potholes. Bikers are the most numerous: imagine killer ants pouring into a narrow trench.

Hamlets are no easier, each a chaos of market stalls, handcarts and livestock, inhabitants either suicidal or insane. Who but a coward would look before crossing the highway? Normal to stop midway to greet a friend. Truck and bus drivers seldom slow. I can't cope. Tension makes me hold too tightly to the controls; my thumbs cramp. Hours on a hard seat and each bump is a knife in the butt. Antibiotics haven't cured my chest. Stop for tea and a crowd gathers to watch me cough. This isn't fun. Depression sets in, exhaustion and fear of failing.

Ten hours brings me finally to Agra – 10 hours to cover 245 kilometres. I can't face navigating the city centre, preferring a hostel in a suburb of tree-shaded streets favoured, in their day, by British officials, and now home to their Indian successors. Set in ample gardens, each white bungalow of Empire bares its white-lettered street sign; occupants have changed, occupations are eternal: collector, engineer, magistrate, chief medical officer. Sentries on side streets show a military presence, as do whitewashed tree trunks and kerbstones, clean gutters, mowed grass.

The hostel is listed in *Lonely Planet* and guests are mostly European (no Indians), late-twenties to mid-forties, few singles. I wait in reception while two Dutch women register. Their room is on the second floor. The stairs are steep. No one offers assistance as they shoulder massive backpacks for the climb. Should I volunteer? Fear holds me back; that, in trying to help, I will make a fool of myself. My own pack is small. My room on the first floor overlooks a central courtyard where a dilatory waiter serves a parody of Western food: chicken sausages made from non-chicken chicken, sliced white bread, processed cheese, coleslaw, ketchup.

Not for me. Sightseeing in the morning so off to bed.

Sleep isn't easy. Old men have to get up in the night. First I stand, hands on the wall, and rise on tiptoe to force the cramp out of my calves. Inch across the slippery bathroom floor. Cough, spit and pee, then back to bed. Lie awake and obsess over how to give up on the project without becoming a laughing stock. More cramp, further need to pee. Not a good night…

Modern Agra is a major industrial city. Traffic-circles and intersections are reminiscent of First World War aerial combat; every pilot picks his own line of attack – go for the gaps, hesitate and lose your tail. Tourists complain of pollution and long queues to visit that monument of Mughal architecture, the Taj Mahal. Back in the sixties, my companion and I were the only visitors to the Taj. I didn't like it. It struck me as a grotesque monument to the male ego: *Marvel at the wealth and power with which I immortalise my love.* And the spindly minarets resemble outsize ballpoint pens, perfect as Christmas stocking fillers for five-year-olds.

Architectural perfection lies across the river in the mausoleum commissioned by Nur Jahan for her parents, the I'timad-ud-Daulah. Human in scale, the mausoleum is of white marble and set in the centre of a square garden of lawns divided by paved paths and water channels. Forty years later, this is again my goal. Gates open at 8 a.m., two gardeners and a gatekeeper, no tourists. I leave my shoes at the foot of the steps leading up to the mausoleum. Sunlight penetrates the central chamber through screens of intricately carved marble. Murals in semi-precious stones depict flowers, fruit, wispy cypress, even wine bottles. The simple tombs lie side by side, a resting place for lovers holding hands, such tender and eternal love.

One of the mausoleum's four gateways overlooks the river. The gateway draws a breeze off the water to create a cool and tranquil place of rest. Washerwomen spread bed sheets to dry on a midstream sandbank. A herdsman drives a dozen buffalo down the far bank. This is the East that I had hoped to find, the East I have missed for so many years. A memory comes of Afghanistan in the early 1980s, a moonlit night, the courtyard of a farmhouse. My companions were mujahideen. We had walked in over the mountains from Pakistan's Tribal Area, crossing a high pass the first day. Russian gunships hunted the border zone and we kept walking all night, much of the time following a dry riverbed. We crossed a second pass soon after dawn and walked all day before sheltering in the farmhouse. I sat against the wall while the young leader of the troop led his men in prayer. The leader noticed me massaging my knees and cracked a joke. His men laughed and a hushed titter of female giggling came from a barred window on the upper floor. Prayers ended, the elderly farmer sat beside me. A younger man brought a hubble-bubble with a chunk of hashish in the bowl on a glowing nest of charcoal. Refusing would have been impolite. We were on the move at dawn. The farmer gave me a horse with instructions to leave it in Pakistan, in Peshawar, where he was well known; someone would bring it back. It was a good horse, content as the rearguard and wise in where to tread on mountain paths.

The Honda showroom in Agra brings me to a different India. The showroom occupies the raised ground floor of an office building next door to a hospital. The owner of both buildings is an Untouchable and the hospital is a charity for Untouchables – those marked by India's caste system as social outcasts. They have been renamed as Dalits as if a name-change could save them. A younger son manages the Honda showroom. We ride an industrial elevator up to meet his father. The office is bare walls, concrete floor, windows with wire screens, no decoration. The father sits behind a low-cost desk armed with a black Bakelite telephone. He is dark, small, intimidating. He is accustomed to obedience: people pay him heed and he talks quietly, though anger is present as he offers me the bare bones of his life, first nodding me to a chair facing the desk.

His father and grandfather were cobblers, not in shops, but working on the sidewalk; knives, needles, thread, scraps of leather, polish, a few rags, all in a wooden box, and an iron cobbler's last. He started the same way. Now his shoe factories export worldwide – yes, to England, he says, and asks my shoe size.

This isn't a man you interrupt. A clerk hovers in the doorway, waiting while the boss talks. His eldest son stands beside the desk. This son studied medicine in Germany, qualified and worked there in a hospital where he met and became engaged to a young Indian doctor. This betrothed was upper caste. News of the engagement reached India. The betrothed's parents were threatened with death. A mob armed with torches gathered outside their family home. I am a writer. This I should report, the truth of India.

Tea is served in small glasses. I am presented with a pair of size 8 black brogues. The doctor son is watching me. He hasn't spoken. He doesn't seem to belong. Dragged back, I think. Sucked down into a quagmire of caste and prejudice. He is a gentler man than his father, quiet, self-contained. Had he enjoyed his years in Germany?

Yes, he says, Germany is a good place to live.

So why doesn't he return? Live what he must have thought of, while in Germany, as a normal life. Free of the caste shit. That last remains unsaid but it is there as our eyes meet.

Family duty is the answer. Imprisoned by duty…

Ashamed of my own freedom, I flee to the safety of *Lonely Planet* land where talk in the hostel's garden courtyard is of India's spiritual- ity, yoga, meditation, mediaeval monuments and medication. I share a table with a Dutch woman, an academic. Her grandfather died of lung cancer and my cough worries her. Am I sure that the cough is bronchitis?

'Quite sure,' I say. 'It's something I get two or three times a year.'

Agra's fort covers 94 acres (UK's Camp Bastion in Afghanistan covers 510). The sandstone walls are 70 feet high and protect a complex of palaces, mosques and courtyards, arched colonnades and pleasure pools (now dry). Here worked the bureaucracy of the Mughal Empire. Now, Agra's citizens crap, do their yoga exercises, picnic and strew their garbage in the pleasure gardens below the walls.

In the great courtyard two small children pose beside their mother while the father takes their picture. My offer to photograph them together is accepted gratefully. They are from Delhi where the husband is CEO of the offshoot of an American software corporation. His days are passed confronting a computer monitor; he loathes computers. The US office opens in the evening at 6.30 Delhi time and he is seldom home before the children are abed. Perhaps not much of a life but it will pay future school and university fees...

I share a charitable enterprise with the Dutch academic whose grandfather died of lung cancer. A friendly rickshaw wallah persuades us to spend the afternoon visiting Agra's tourist shops. Rickshaw wallahs are paid a commission on each tourist they bring to a shop, this whether the tourist makes a purchase or not. We buy nothing. The rickshaw wallah earns a week's income.

In the evening I cruise the neighbourhood and find a cheap restaurant. A tall man with fierce grey beard sits alone at the adjoining table. He asks my nationality before introducing himself as a retired lieutenant colonel. He talks of honour – or lack of honour – in today's society. Lack of honour is destroying India. Ninety per cent of Indians are corrupt. More than 90 per cent, 98 per cent, so he assures me.

Of his two brothers, one is a full colonel, the other a general. Both brothers have large houses, cars with drivers, children at private school. He recount his arguments with these brothers, their pleading that he should be reasonable. His response, that there is no honour in reasonable, that he has acted honourably always.

'So now I am living in a small room and eating in such places,' he says with a dismissive wave at our surroundings. 'Everywhere it is the same. Look at you British. You were always honourable. Now see what is happening with you. This Blair with his lies. England's reputation is destroyed.'

He suffers from stomach pains (presumably an ulcer) and eats only dahl with curd. He departs, very upright, very military in his bearing. An honourable man, he must have been the subordinate from Hell. I imagine his brothers pleading with him over the years to refrain from arguing just once, to drift just once with the official current, if not for his own good, for the good of the family. Never!

My own army service as a subaltern in a cavalry regiment suffered its ups and downs – mostly downs. The major commanding our squadron was a kind and charming man and competent at giving orders that came from elsewhere. The smallest of counter-suggestions unnerved him. 'Don't argue,' was his defence. To which I would get as far as, 'But…' before came his almost panicked riposte: 'No, Simon! Don't dare even open your mouth.'

Two days in Agra is enough. Gwalior is 110 kilometres south on an excellent highway. Traffic is sparse and 70 kph is comfortable. I grow in confidence and make good time between villages across a land of flat fields of yellow mustard. The terrain changes midway. Millennia of monsoons have gouged twisting gulches between pinnacles of grey-red earth tufted with sparse scrub. Or was it thousands of men and women endlessly picking at clay to feed the kilns?

Tumbled walls of a fortress cap a long ridge. What in this ghastly land is there to protect? Yet, suddenly, to the left on the old road appears a bridge of seven pointed Islamic arches in red brick, delicate spires at each end, pepper pots in the middle. Beautiful!

Then three men on a strange pilgrimage: thin men, barefoot and dressed only in dhotis. They have two cushions. The first lies on his cushion. The second drops his cushion ahead of the prostrate pilgrim and prostrates himself. The first rises and passes his cushion to the third man who lies down ahead of the second man. And so it continues up the dual carriageway. How far are they going? From whence have they come? Curse this lack of a common language…

Gwalior sprawls as do all Indian towns and cities. The fortress commands the town from high on a solitary plateau three kilometres in length. Towering walls of intricately carved sandstone glow in the sunlight. Entry is barred by massive wooden doors that could give passage to a pair of elephants with howdahs. I duck through a small portal for pedestrians. A guide at the ticket office accompanies me back to my bike and lifts the bike in over the door's foot, then invites me to a cup of sweet tea.

A museum of sculptures ranging from the first century to the seventeenth is a delight. Of the Man Sing Palace, the top floor is closed and crumbling. Down a floor and the rooms are hewn stone and pillars opening to courtyards, small in scale and unimpressive. The truth of the palace lies below in unlit layers carved from the rock and connected through narrow twisting stairways and through dog-leg doorways and corridors down which no man, however thin, could pass another. Such was the palace, surely a dark sinister creation of regal paranoia – or excavated as a cool retreat from the summer heat? Or did the dank walls and darkness speak of fettered prisoners blinded by years without light? Tortured, did their wounds fester? Did they scrabble for the carcass of a dead rat?

As always, in India, the choice lies with the beholder.

I remark to a probable English speaker, middle-aged, with the look of an intellectual, on the difficulty of imagining how it once was. He replies that it will be gone in 50 years, destroyed by neglect and by the corruption of those charged with its care.

An invitation to coffee at the Indian Coffee House in downtown Gwalior comes from two middle-aged advisers from the Ministry of

Education, Delhi. I remark on the language handicap for a traveller trying to understand India. One of my hosts replies that Indians are complicated. They are friends for a thousand years, then in a moment, slaughter each other – slaughter without reason – only because some politician says they should.

His companion insists on the extraordinary advances over the past 10 years, the number of cars, millions of mobile telephones. Even the caste system, he says. He himself knows Untouchables in high positions. Even the Minister for Justice is an Untouchable. Now that Untouchables are in power, they are the most corrupt. A hundred times worse. Their turn has come. It is human nature to use such opportunity.

His companion says that the British were always more honourable. Now Blair has destroyed that reputation. Such a liar. It would take centuries for the British to recover.

Yes, Blair again. So it was on my travels throughout Hispanic America and in the most unlikely and diverse of company, this frequent condemnation of the United Kingdom's recently retired prime minister.

The Jai Villas Palace was built at the Maharajah of Gwalior's command in the 1870s in what is now the centre of Gwalior town. The architect, Lieutenant Colonel Michael Filose, was an English Catholic whose family had served the Maharajahs of Gwalior since the seventeenth century. The palace is a vast white Italianate fantasy.

The Maharajah built the Usha Kiran Palace in the same parkland to house the Prince and Princess of Wales who visited Gwalior for a few days while touring India in the early 1900s. The Taj Group has transformed the Usha Kiran into one of the world's most delightful hotels and I am a very lucky old man – the front manager has emailed me an invitation to breakfast. The manager is a history graduate. Breakfast conversation begins with motorbikes, progresses via religion in history to God as love, family and the insanity dictating much of the region's politics – splendid accompaniment to a fruit salad and black coffee. Then back on the road…

Janasi is the next major town south, 95 kilometres. A dual carriageway is under construction. Stretches of the old road have been
ripped apart. Renewed stretches are deep gravel waiting for tar and
diversions are rutted dirt. I hate dirt and I hate gravel. Dust clouds
envelop crazed bus drivers in their fight for primacy. Dumper trucks
are as scary as maddened elephants. My little Honda slips and slith-
ers. This is not a fun ride, yet elderly bikers speed by, no helmets,
beards henna-red with dust; insouciant women ride pillion, faces
veiled, an infant or two clutched in their arms. This is their nor-
mality. It is not mine. I want to be somewhere else. Anywhere else.
Terror is a lousy companion…

Roadworks end. I am back on tar. Tar is my natural habitat. Fear
drains away. I relax. The morning's conversation at the Usha Kiran
has left an afterglow and I am enjoying myself. The sweet humid
scent of cane fields carries memories of my years in Cuba, as do
overladen trailers swaying towards a sugar central. Two men work
at the top of an electricity pylon. Hard hats? Safety belts? Don't be
silly, this is India; men are replaceable. So how dare I complain? A
mile left of the road, two massive temples dominate a small town. A
further few miles and a white wedding cake of a palace overlooks a
small lake. To investigate or not is the dilemma. India is strewn with
magical buildings. Driving through Rajasthan in convoy all those
years ago we stopped everywhere. I was young. Time seemed infinite.

Janasi is charmless industrial and to be avoided. Four roads
intersect to create a maelstrom of carts, cars, buses, trucks, tractors,
trailers, tuktuks and a billion bikers bent on suicide. I am sandwiched
between two minibuses. Please God, I don't want to die – not yet.

The maelstrom spits me out on to the road south. A fork to the
right a few kilometres beyond Janasi leads to the small princely
state of Orchha. The countryside changes instantly from dry, flat
and dusty to a gentle switchback of small green fields and green-
leaf woodland. The road skirts a single-platform railway station, the
crossing guarded by a swing barrier. A gateway that has lost its gates
breaches massive walls of dry-set rock. Beyond the arch lies what was

Maharajah Orchha's private domain. A tall archway and gatehouse guard the gravel drive leading to the Maharajah's hunting lodge (so reports my guidebook) and the Hotel Bundelkhand Riverside.

The hotel is a cloistered rectangle surmounted by slender-pillared cupolas. Built on a gentle slope, the cloister encloses, on the lower level, a lawned garden divided into four quarters by low hedges. An ancient shrine in crumbling brick stands beside a small swimming pool on the upper level. The cloister walls are pale ochre, pillars and arches a deep terracotta outlined in white. Red and white bougainvillea and pale plumbago drape the arches while trees shade the surrounds of the pool terrace and carpet the grass with pink blossom.

Ten minutes of polite room-rate negotiations prove successful. A servant leads me across the lawn to an ample bedroom. French shutters open to a small balcony overlooking the Betwa River with low thick jungle beyond. A ride of less than 100 kilometres and I am exhausted, caked with dust, chest heaving, a slight case of the runs. Now for a hot shower in a vast marble bathroom, walls patterned in blue and white tiles and towels thick and big as a winter blanket. Such are the true joys of travel...

Guests gather on the lawn before dinner in a circle of easy chairs round an open fire. Turbaned musicians play classical Indian music and sing softly. The hotel manager introduces me to a captain in the Indian Army Air Corps and to a young couple (architects) from LA with a baby daughter; his parents emigrated from Pakistan, Muslim; hers were from India, Hindu. The daughter will have interesting choices. A young relative of the Maharajah is waiting for news of the approaching train for Delhi. A keen biker (Enfield Bullet and new Yamaha 250), he criticises tourists for visiting only the fringes of the subcontinent and ignoring India's heartland. He extols a ride through gloriously forested hills where streams tumble into crystal pools. The stationmaster telephones news of the train's approach – no time for me to write down the magic route.

I am seated for dinner at a table of fellow foreigners, amongst them a young American NGO married to a yoga-teaching Ukrainian. They are on holiday from Cambodia where he manages the office of a conservation trust while she has founded a nursery school. Their daughter (five?) sits beside me, her opening remark that her dog has died. The dog, so she recounts, was untrainable and pooped and weed in the house so was kept in the yard. The vet prescribed the dog the wrong medicine. Given the dog's habits, possibly the right medicine? And poops, pee and dead dogs make for unfortunate conversation when faced by a wet curry and suffering from the runs…

Opposite sits an attractive but mostly silent Japanese woman (Miyuki from Tokyo), probably in her mid-thirties. Her travelling companion, Francis, is younger. Hungarian, he was educated in Germany and has built a house outside Sharm el-Sheikh, Egypt, where he owns a PADI dive school. He and Miyuki are escapees from an ashram in Kerala and are travelling on Francis's ancient and much modified Enfield Bullet motorcycle. Francis is a somewhat tense young man, fidgety hands, and fast emptying a bottle of single malt whisky. Perhaps he should have stayed a little longer at the ashram.

Miyuki from Tokyo heads for bed to nurse a head cold. Francis brings his single malt to my room. He sits on my bed, bottle in one hand, tumbler in the other, and details his fears of an imminent heart attack. Pains in his chest began shortly after the death of his father the previous year, of course from a heart attack. The fear has accompanied Francis ever since, in the first months so severe that he was unable to leave the house. He suspects that the chest pains are psychosomatic, or wishes to believe so; yet, unconvinced, seeks medical advice – though, as a precaution, deliberately chooses doctors whose diagnosis he can discount. At this point in his tale I bolt for the bathroom and drop my pants with a millisecond to spare. The first spasm doubles me up and I tumble off the throne seat in mid-defecation. I shout to Francis that he must leave and begin sluicing the bathroom and washing myself.

The bathroom is clean. I am clean. I rest at peace in the big bed. Black beams divide the ceiling into four. Each segment is hand-painted with a freeze of green leaves, a vase of flowers in each corner and a pattern of pointed arches down the centre. Midnight in Orchha, early evening in England. I telephone my wife, B.

How is she, I ask.

Fine, she says.

How am I, she asks.

Fine, I say.

My first morning in Orchha and I have discovered paradise. For the past hour I have been sitting on my bedroom balcony and watching dawn spread across the river. A pale mist lies across the water and the jungle on the far bank; not a mist of carbon monoxide, a natural morning mist. Water tumbling over a low weir and over boulders is the only sound. The sun, orange-gold in the mist, rises out of the jungle. An elderly Indian dressed in baggy black cotton shirt and pants walks down to the river and, kneeling, washes his hands before raising them to the sun in prayer. He turns, sees me, and, hands together, dips his head in greeting. He disappears up the steps to the courtyard garden only to return and, standing below my balcony, reaches up to offer two saffron-petalled flowers. So, yes, paradise. True, my bowels are loose and I am coughing up my lungs; I can deal with that. I will dress in a little while, sit in the garden and order dry toast and black coffee for breakfast. Ahead lies a wonderful day of exploration. Orchha boasts three abandoned sixteenth- and seventeenth-century palaces, three superb temples and the ruling family's cenotaphs.

Dew on the lawn sparkles in the rising sun. Small birds dart and dive amongst the blossoms drooping from the shrine on the pool terrace. A striped squirrel watches as I sip my coffee. I watch two women squatting to sweep the gravel path, gold nose rings, togas of senatorial purple, bare feet.

The young architects from California, slim and beautiful, make a perfect pair as they stroll across the lawn. She cradles their baby in her arms. They lack the self-consciousness frequent in the beautiful of other lands; in California, beauty is commonplace. California is where they belong.

He tells me of visiting Pakistan, of his family there, liberal intellectuals, well travelled, many educated abroad. Ten years ago a bar in an upstairs room would have been standard at a family wedding, whisky, beer, the sexes mixed. Now fear of denunciation rules; sexes segregated, women of his own family veiled.

His wife, a Hindu, speaks of her fear at their coming visit – and he that this will be their final trip. Nor will they visit India again; to do so without visiting Pakistan would be insulting and hurtful to his family.

The baby needs changing. They return to their room. I slip my sandals off. The dew on the grass is deliciously cool between my toes. The waiter brings fresh coffee. In such tranquillity, fanaticism and its violence is momentarily unimaginable.

A glorious day of exploration accompanying Miyuki and Francis.

Orchha was founded by the Rajput Rajas of Bundela in 1501. Orchha town is a village. Three famous temples make it a place of pilgrimage. A crumbling and long-abandoned Customs house marks the entrance; a thief has been stealing the handmade bricks from the rear wall.

The main street is low houses mostly whitewashed, a few small shops and a bank. At the end is the temple square where a cluster of shacks serve street food to pilgrims in their saffron robes, foreheads anointed with a splodge of ochre ghee. The causeway to the left crosses a dry moat to a rock promontory within a bend of the Betwa River. Three towering sandstone palaces command the promontory. Every room and every courtyard is designed to capture and channel the cooling breeze off the water; no need for energy-devouring air conditioning here; what an example for modern architects…Though three palaces only separated by a paved courtyard seems overkill for such a tiny princely state.

The Jahangiri Mahal is the best maintained – or the least decayed. The square base is an unscaleable fortress. Above rise two layers of open casements carved from sandstone, mini cupolas at each corner. These two levels support the Maharajah's chambers and surround a central courtyard. Domed pleasure pavilions stand at each corner and midway along each side. Cupolas on slender pillars surround the domes. Each dome and cupola is surmounted by a spike – a comical reminder of nineteenth-century Prussian army helmets, the *Pickel-haube*. Not something I mention to Francis who scampers up and down flight after flight of narrow, crumbling stairs with the agility of a mountain goat. Miyuki and I are more circumspect. The dead drop from the open casements makes us nervous. So do the vultures that wheel above the domes only waiting for us to drop a sandwich – or better yet, drop dead. They swoop and land in the adjoining room to where we stand, they spitting obscenities at each other, the claw of their talons harsh on the stone casement edge. The crows are less malevolent.

My guidebook reports that the upper levels of the palace contain 132 rooms with a further 132 rooms below in the windowless fortress. I don't count. Here lived and worked the bureaucrats of State, scores of servants, palace guards, the Maharajah's wives and children, innumerable relatives. Now only emptiness remains, every room stripped to the bare stone. The emptiness is depressing, the lack of any furniture or colour other than a few remaining lapis tiles on the frieze edging the pleasure domes. Difficult to imagine it in all its splendour...

At least, in Agra, tourists crowded the courts and squares, Indians proudly relishing their nation's history. Here is a single Indian family: the enthusiastic father, clerk class perhaps, or schoolteacher, three pens clipped in the breast pocket of his white cotton shirt, fake-leather sandals, recites a running commentary as he drags a reluctant and sulking pre-teen son from room to room. The boy's shawled mother follows, silent, humble, obedient.

We three are the only foreigners. We have our tickets and we have our guidebooks in English, German and Japanese. We are in the exploratory stage of what may become a friendship and content in each other's company. Stop for a moment and a mid-aged guide dressed in grubby white forces himself between us. A torrent of incomprehensible explanations pours from him. Is he paid by the word/minute as Indian bus drivers are by the passenger mile? Perhaps he has a bus driver brother. The spittle on his lips is off-putting...

'Please go away,' we plead in English, German and Japanese – to no effect.

My attempt at bribery merely encourages him.

Francis tries, 'Piss off!'

The guide stops in mid-cascade. I, burdened by guilt of Empire, press a further 10 rupees into his hand. And turn to meet a look of near hatred on the face of the clerk-class Indian father. A puff of breeze spins tiny towers of sandstone powder across the inner court-yard. Ah, well...

One palace is sufficient for Miyuki who sits below on a stone bench in the sun and snuffles sadly into Kleenex. She is the first patient to have undergone a new and life-saving surgical procedure. If she wanted me to know for what ailment she would tell me; asking would be presumptuous. My chest infection in non-contagious. So I hope. Odd thoughts to have, me seated beside Miyuki now and exhausted after scaling a second palace, though not all the way to the top of the highest pavilion where Francis pirouettes on the very edge of the helmet's brim, nothing to save him from oblivion. A death wish? Escape from his fear of cardiac arrest? Mad...

The breeze off the river almost dispels the burnt oil and spice scent from the fast-food counters in the temple square and from the garbage strewn in the moat. Miyuki's perfume is tinged with eucalyp-tus tincture for her cold. She is small and neat of figure with a gentle sadness that demands to be comforted. She is in her mid-thirties and beautiful. I am an overweight septuagenarian. She is travelling with Francis. Reaching for her hand would be inappropriate.

I am saved from unseemly desire by a mini mob of primary-school children exploding in from the ticket barrier. Their teacher begs for discipline. The school must be fee-paying; a state schoolteacher would bellow and whack heads. Francis descends and we leave for the temples.

The Ram Raja Temple was built in the sixteenth century by order of Maharajah Madhukar Shah and is dedicated to Lord Ram. The temple is vast, formal rather than ornate, and besieged by tourists who crowd the centre courtyard. Lord Ram sits with his left leg folded back on his right thigh. Pilgrims jostle for sight of his left big toe. See the toe and your wish will be granted (maybe).

In total contrast is the Chaturbhuj Temple whose ornate spires spiritually subjugate the town and its palaces. Basted in carvings, the exterior is Hindu architecture as foreign tourists expect. The overall form is different, somehow more disciplined, familiar. Steps mount a massive stone base. Enter and I am in a Gothic cathedral. Stone pillars support the towering nave. Twin wings form the cruciform. Altars are missing and the casement unglazed. We three tourists are alone in the immense empty space. Dark and sombre and extraordinary...

I imagine wooden pews, stained glass, a high altar with golden crucifix and candlesticks, bishop in his embroidered vestments turning to bless the congregation.

The view from the hill overlooking the town gives a clearer perspective: twin spires at the end corners of the cathedral arms, dome surmounting the entrance end of the main nave, towering spire above the altar. The memory comes slowly, an autumn day, Toledo in Spain. The colour is different: Orchha's temple is pale honey sandstone, Toledo's cathedral granite grey. But the architect, the concept, there has to be a connection. Ideas travelled and the dates fit, Toledo earlier by a century.

No reason to burden Miyuki and Francis with my fancies; they are in the 'India is unique' stage of their journey while I have been reading the diaries that recount the sojourn in Delhi of a Moroccan traveller of the mid-fourteenth century, Ibn Battuta. A true adventurer...

Ghats are wide stone steps leading down the bank of lake or river. Soap in hand, multitudes of India's bathers come in the early morning. Late afternoon on the Betwa River, I share the view with a single family. Beyond the ghat stand squat towers, domed turrets at each corner and a central spire. The moss-covered stone is a deep chocolate tinged with orange by the setting sun. Such were the intricately moulded jellies served at the grand dinner tables of Victoria's Empire: these are the cenotaphs of Orchha's Maharajahs. A car parks behind me. A young man walks to the edge of the ghat: short hair, white sports shirt, razor-creased chinos, polished boat shoes, certainly an English speaker. We watch a while in silence the river flow.

Then, 'Beautiful,' I remark.

'Yes,' he says, and that he was wondering whether the river would exist in 10 or 20 years.

'Global warming?'

'Yes, climates change…'

I enquire as to his profession. Soldier is his initial reply – under further prodding, officer commanding a missile regiment. So surely with a science degree and at least one Masters. Not your standard army officer, but someone well able to judge whether climate change is fact or fiction.

He seems to me very young to be a colonel. Even a lieutenant colonel. I watch as he walks back to a small spotless Suzuki jeep, canvas cover furled. The uniformed driver, equally smart, salutes and opens the passenger door. The young colonel nods to me and they drive away. I ride back to drinks on the lawn with Francis and Miyuki at the Bundelkhand Riverside.

Christmas Eve, 6:30 a.m. and upright tufts of thin mist float downstream along the far bank of the Betwa River. I imagine a leopard, belly brushing the fallen leaves as it slinks beneath the trees. Perhaps a tiger's guttural cough. I have never seen a tiger in the wild. A memory comes of lions sprawled lazing in the sun on the bare side of a ridge above the camel track leading to my camp in Ethiopia's Ogaden Province. An ancient memory – nearly 60 years.

The sun rises out of the jungle. A lone bird flies upstream, perhaps a cormorant. I must pack and load the bike. Taj Hotels have invited me to spend Christmas at the Usha Kiran Palace in Gwalior. The road is familiar so the ride will be easier than was the ride down to Orchha. Memories of the lions will make for good company.

Francis rides north with me to Gwalior on his ancient Enfield Bullet, Miyuki on the pillion. The Enfield is slow and Francis mistrusts the engine. He worries that it is overheating, stops often; in the saddle, listens for malfunction, head cocked to the right and low. Meanwhile Miyuki is silent, only her eyes visible below her helmet. A pale blue scarf printed with tiny flowers covers the rest of her face. Gloves protect her hands.

In such company, my Honda Stunner seems a frisky racehorse as it bucks and bounces on the potholed diversions alongside the unfinished highway. It is more stable in the dirt than the Honda Cargo I rode the length of the Americas. I feel more confident in the saddle and the electric start is bliss – though, as expected, the seat is a pain in the butt.

We stop for tea twice on the road and go our separate ways in Gwalior's city centre, Miyuki and Francis continuing north to Agra for Christmas. I will join them on Boxing Day – if I am alive. A similar scarf to Miyuki's would have kept the dust out of my lungs.

Christmas Day and I am sick as a pig. I have been awake much of the night with my chest pretending to be an ancient harmonium. I am housed at the Usha Kiran Palace in an interconnecting suite furnished with an emperor-sized bed, two 44-inch TVs, a white leather couch that stretches from here to eternity, two white leather armchairs and a long coffee table bearing a vast bowl of fresh fruit and a vase of flowers. Windows to the east catch the morning sun across a wide lawn. To the north French windows open to my private patio where, were this summer, I could loll on a stone bench in the evening and perhaps imagine myself very grand. For now I make do with a pre-breakfast bubble bath – though perhaps bath is a misnomer; this is a granite and mosaic pool into which I climb two marble steps.

The steam eases my chest and I call my beloved B in England. Our eldest son, Joshua, is home for Christmas and B is roasting a boned duck for their dinner. Next call is to my daughter, Anya, in Duchess County, NY – snow and a turkey. Finally my grandson, Charlie, three years old, son of my eldest son from my first marriage. My brother and sister-in-law have given Charlie a large wigwam. Charlie has insisted that it be erected immediately in the living room of my son's small London apartment. My son and his partner are in the tent. Charlie, very excited, shrieks what might be a greeting.

And so to a late breakfast.

The executive chef at the Usha Kiran Palace has cured my chest with frequent pots of herbal tea; the recipe is his mother's. Steaming myself in the bubble bath every few hours may have helped. And three nights of sybaritic comfort. Mostly I have stayed in my suite, nursing myself while watching cricket on television. Foreign guests have been cordial, Indian guests less so. Evening gatherings round the fire on the lawn at the Bundelkhand Riverside brought us together and the manager made introductions: the young architects from California, the doctor in charge of research at Bhopal and his wife, a retired air marshal and his family.

The Indian guests at the Usha Kiran seem to me to come of a different class. More moneyed. Blatantly so … And less welcoming of a foreigner. Dismissive even. Now my bags are packed, bike loaded. Finally I face the perennial worry of the traveller in a new country as to how much to tip. An Indian guest in a viciously expensive raw silk suit and gold Rolex Oyster is paying his bill with a platinum credit card at the reception desk. I ask what tip would be normal for a room steward. 'There's no need' is the reply. So much for the joys of Christmas…

4
AGRA AND WESTWARD THROUGH RAJASTHAN

I am carrying too much gear. First on to the pillion goes my grey plastic suitcase (extending handle and wheels). My laptop is wrapped in a bath towel and rests on a bed of underclothes in the lower half of the case, rolled socks and T-shirts as side protection. Smart clothes go in the upper half. A spider's web of bungee rubbers holds the case in place. Further bungee rubbers hold a small backpack on top of the suitcase. Shoes go in the left side pannier, reference books in the other. The magnetic tank bag holds map, guidebook, sponge bag and medication. I'm wearing cords with long johns, vest, shirt, two jumpers and a leather bomber jacket purchased at the market of a small town on Peru's Altiplano for 40 dollars. Not smart…

A Harley or Honda Goldwing might be permissible in the Usha Kiran Palace car park, possibly the biggest of BMWs – 125s are an embarrassment. Particularly when laced with umpteen bungee rubbers. My Stunner waits in the shade beside a flower bed raised against the perimeter wall. A splendidly uniformed guard, my equally splendid room steward and two gardeners have come to watch me mount. I try for nonchalance: a quick smile for all and swing the left leg over the gear. The leg won't swing that high. So much for nonchalance.

The gardeners lift the bike round against the raised flower bed. The steward steadies me as I mount the flower bed's retaining parapet. Over goes the leg and I settle myself on the saddle. The room steward hands me my helmet much as a Plantagenet squire might to a knight at the jousts. Press the button and the engine purrs. The guard salutes and off I wobble in search of the National Highway to Agra. Of course I get lost; Indian cities are confusing.

Once found, the six-lane National Highway is a joy when compared with the road from Orchha. The Stunner can cruise happily at 90 kph. I am comfortable at 70. My confidence is growing. I feel safe and pay greater attention to my fellow road users. Not all are homicidal, though drivers never indicate. Trucks and cars stick to the outside lanes. Indian bikers overtake on the inside. Squeezed by an erratic truck driver, they take to the hard shoulder. Women sit side saddle, faces framed in flapping head shawls, at least one child in their lap. A further child or two sit astride the gas tank. Perhaps one in 50 men wears a helmet. Women and children, never.

I stop midway for tea at a typical truck stop, open-fronted beneath a flat roof. An upright Coca-Cola cooler holds pride of place, fly-specked electric cable dangling from a hook screwed into a ceiling encrusted with smoked grease. The range is a dozen clay nests of smouldering charcoal on a brick base. The cook in stained dhoti officiates over fat-bellied cauldrons, karahi woks, flat chapati irons and a pair of huge kettles. Tables and chairs are wood-and-nails carpentry, a few string beds at the back.

This is strictly a truck and biker place. Cars speed by...

My rules for self-preservation: tea or bottled water (check the cap), no meat, no raw salad. The scent of spiced dahl is seductive. With curd? Definitely. And two chapatis, please. Total cost? Negligible...

Tomorrow is the end of Islam's holy month of Muharram, a day of great celebration for Shia Muslims. Francis and Miyuki are staying in the old city. Francis has reserved me a room in the same guest house. Lanes are narrow and crowded with Shia men dancing and shouting the name of the martyred Hassan ibn Ali, grandson of the Prophet. Easing through without offending demands many smiles, much politeness and great patience.

The guest house is the bottom end of bottom-end *Lonely Planet*. My room has the smell of a mushroom tunnel that's suffered a plague. The window at one end overlooks the junction of two lanes, no netting on the window and no mosquito net over the bed. Stains on the mattress are visible through the thin nylon sheet and cockroaches are holding the national jamboree in the bathroom. The shower dribbles, hand basin grimy, a glance at the lavatory and I retch. The only possible excuse for this hellhole is the view of the Taj Mahal from the rooftop restaurant. A film crew is shooting a television advertisement, lovers leaning against the parapet, Taj in the background. A young man from the advertising agency, linen jacket over sports shirt, chinos, polished shoes and a clipboard, watches as the director rehearses the young actors. A gofer brings lemon sodas on a tray from outside and they take a break.

A knack of entering into conversation is essential for travel writers. The ad agency executive surveys the lean-to kitchen at the rear of the roof terrace where a kitchen helper squats to rinse plates in an aluminium bowl by the roof drain, barefoot, grimy vest.

'How can you people eat in this place?' the ad exec asks as he inspects the foreigners, mostly young, seated at the tables.

'I don't,' I say, which is a minimalist Saint Peter moment, though the street noise would drown a cock's crow.

No hiding the ad exec's distaste as a woman holds his attention, narrow-faced with pale red frizzy hair pulled back and tied with an elastic band. She is almost flat-chested beneath a white cotton waistcoat loosely fastened with ties. Necklace is a few beads on a black string; baggy Ali Baba harem pants of faded saffron cotton, the hem pulled up between her legs and tucked into the waistband. The waistcoat is narrow and leaves her shoulders bare. She is leaning forward across the table to study her companion's guidebook. Elbows out displays the hair in her armpits. The hair is dark with sweat – in my mind, ugly whether in women or men. Perhaps this is a generation thing – though the ancient Greeks shaved their armpits, as did the Romans. Her companion's head is shaven, identical waistcoat, grubby white pyjama pants, sex indeterminate.

One night and I am moving on, a night of cursing Francis for booking us here. Drums beat at every corner from dusk till dawn while eight loudspeakers directly outside my bedroom blare the incessant chant: Hassan Hussein, Hassan Hussein. Sleep impossible, I watch from my window a ballet of whirling stick-fights at the junction of the two lanes and wonder that Islam's schism should have followed so closely on the Prophet's death.

Morning brings a procession of handcarts winding up the lane towards the Taj Mahal. Small boys dressed in pristine white with white skullcaps sit on the carts, proud architects of model mosques made from coloured wrapping paper. Dad and older brothers push; drum and trumpet bands provide the music. Women are back home as God designed, cooking, cleaning, doing the laundry and washing-up.

A walk down the procession exchanging five with the boys and admiring their artwork, then pack the bike and follow Francis and Miyuki out of town. Francis has decided on a short cut that takes us through the centre of a seemingly endless market. A national holiday and every man, woman and child is on the street plus goats, donkeys, holy cows, the occasional elephant and a few camels. Two up on the heavier Enfield provides a momentum and the engine's commanding burble clears a path. The Honda is almost silent and I am scared of hitting someone, of an infuriated mob. The confidence I gained on yesterday's ride to Agra evaporates. I can't cope. This is final. I'm too old. Simply abandoning the bike in the middle of the market is a negative so I creep forward with innumerable stops. Half an hour of this before the crowd thins. Francis has stopped and is waiting for me for the umpteenth time. I apologise for being so slow. I don't confess to being exhausted, for wanting to pack it in and go home. We are aiming for Fatehpur Sikri, less than 50 kilometres. The road is good tar, not too much traffic. Maybe I can survive for another day.

Last night Muharram at a *Lonely Planet* doss house in Agra, tonight a Tibetan-owned guest house. A national holiday and Fatehpur Sikri has been invaded by holidaymakers. All standard accommodation is either full or trebled in price. A kindly local cop directs Francis down a dirt footpath beneath the fortress walls and across a stinking refuse tip to a small group of cottages that has tried and failed to grow into a village for the past few hundred years. The Sunset guest house is a new-build and cheap. My room is large, bathroom clean and the welcome warm. Our fellow guests are a little weird.

You probably need to be a little weird to seek a guest house the far side of a refuse tip. However, weird is a subjective judgement. I consider riding a tandem pedal bike from Barcelona weird. The riders are Argentinian. They probably think me weird, septuagenarian on a teenager's café racer. Nor are Francis and Miyuki on an antique Enfield a standard couple – plus the very tall, skeletal French couple communicating in plaintive whispers.

The French husband combines careers as a commercially unsuccessful musician and reluctant sound engineer in the French film industry. The wife does something artistic with puppets (not a biggie in the earning stakes) and no doubt spends hours cooking taste-free vegetarian meals (why am I so bitchy?). They have been on a duty visit to the Frenchman's mother who escaped to a Buddhist monastery 15 years back. This is the Frenchman's third trip to India and he loathes pretty much everything – particularly the food. His wife is a novice. Travelling by bus has thrown her into mental shock and chilli has done for her belly.

For those who admire intricate stone carving, Fatehpur Sikri is superb. Building of the citadel commenced in the 1570s at the command of the Mughal Emperor Akbar. As emperors go, Akbar was a liberal. Of his three favourite wives, one was Turkish Muslim, one a Hindu princess and the third a Christian from Goa. Of all the citadel, the Diwan-i-Khas (Hall of Private Audience) is most remarkable. Here Akbar sat on a throne raised high on a pillar and debated with philosophers of every faith. The philosophers sat in a circular gallery connected to the throne by four bridges. The pillar head is lotus-shaped while the pillar is carved with motifs: Muslim, Hindu, Christian and Buddhist. Akbar is one of two protagonists in Salman Rushdie's perceptive, gentle and witty novel, *The Moor's Last Sigh*. Read and enjoy…

The researcher for *Lonely Planet* suggests that Akbar sentenced criminals (a loose term under all-powerful rulers, whether emperors, kings, fascist dictators or secretary-generals of the communist party) to be trampled to death by his favourite elephant. According to *Lonely Planet*, Akbar enjoyed watching. A stone tower decorated with hundreds of stone elephant tusks is said to be Akbar's memorial to the elephant (surely nicknamed Crunch Crunch?). The *Footprint Handbook*, though perhaps more prosaic, is more reliable in matters historical. Both have excellent descriptions of the citadel while *Eyewitness* contains the best illustrations (this is a personal opinion). Yes, I travel with three guidebooks and the brilliantly researched *India: A History* by Keay...

While peacefully wandering the citadel, I am accosted by a small pugnacious Indian gentleman wearing a pale green suit and a felt elf hat.

'What do you think of this?' he demands without preamble or introduction. 'Is it beautiful? Have you been in England? Have you visited Hampton Court? That is beauty. Built the same time as this. I know. I am history graduate.'

I attempt the smallest protest – surely we should imagine the citadel as it was: courtyards spread with carpet and cooled by fountains, every channel filled with water, pots planted with lemon trees and pomegranates, sweet scented roses, beautiful maidens in embroidered silk...

'No, no, no – that is all only decoration with no importance. Hampton Court is not needing imagination...'

We meet again later in the afternoon. The elf hat immediately launches a fresh attack on Akbar's citadel. He is accompanied by a tall well-built thirty-something to whom I plead, 'You have to listen to this?'

'Listen?' he says in one of those wondrously casual upmarket English Home Counties voices. 'I've had to listen for three weeks. He's my dad.'

Seven thirty a.m. on the roof terrace at the Sunset guest house, Fatehpur Sikri. In the valley below, a thin mist lies across pale green fields bordered by trees. The Nepalese owner of the guest house feeds birds each morning on a smaller terrace. Five green parakeets watch me from the parapet while six striped squirrels scavenge for yesterday's seeds. Doves wheel above the trees. Shrill children's voices argue with mothers in the nearly village, a drum beats in town. Here, on the hill, the sun burns through the mist and warms my fingers as I type. Staff appear rubbing sleep from their eyes. 'Breakfast, Uncle?'

Breakfast would be great: coffee, masala omelette, toast.

The lower end of the fortress is now a faint grey line of stone teeth and the mist gentles the ghastly tower monument to Crunch Crunch.

The owner spreads seed on the bird terrace. Sparrows are first to the feast followed by a grey-necked crow, now 20 or more parakeets. The parakeets are argumentative and drown out the village voices. The staff have a fire burning outside the kitchen. Wood smoke faintly scents the air. Breakfast arrives. The diffident French couple come to table, muffled and gentle-voiced. Next the Argentinian tandem bicyclist to drape laundry on the rail. Francis briefly surfaces to report that he is only running 10 minutes late for our proposed 9 o'clock departure for Jaipur.

On such a glorious morning, timetables are for the birds.

Fatehpur Sikri to Jaipur is 260 kilometres west on the six-lane National Highway 11. The Enfield is painfully slow on the open road. The Honda is frisky. My confidence rebuilds. I am amused rather than terrified by drivers' disregard for the law. Why get angry at two oncoming trucks abreast on our side of the central reservation? Or become incensed by the tractor driver towing a trailer who does a U-turn? Every gas station exit is strewn with broken glass; this is India where only cowards look before pulling out.

Francis breaks for lunch midday at a small market town. Fast-food sellers flourish along the roadside, rusting tin roofs propped up on skinny wooden posts; cauldrons simmer over charcoal, a couple of crude wooden benches out front. Miyuki and I risk the chai that comes in glasses rinsed in a kerosene can of dubious water. Francis, insanely adventurous, munches onion bhajis. A crowd gathers, questions as to who we are, where we are going. English is basic. Amplification serves the interlocutors. The crowd excites Francis to further perils: lentil rissoles, supremely dangerous stewed goat meat, curd and a chapati. A man with a big moustache and a red turban sits his small son on the Stunner. I am to stand beside the boy on one side, dad on the other. Photographs are taken. Francis is grinning at all and sundry while giving little self-congratulatory waves of his hands – as a climber might after ascending the Matterhorn. Miyuki has shrunk into her head cold. If she talks at all, it is whispered monosyllables. Two camels heavily laden with bricks plod by. We remount and, strong on self-preservation, look left and right before rejoining the highway.

Francis worries that the Enfield is overheating. He waves me alongside to listen to the engine. How does it sound? Like Enfields sound. Imagine the deep gurgles as a thirsty German drinks his first litre at the Munich beer festival.

Joyous of miracles or a mirage is a CaféDay road stop in the middle of nowhere. CaféDays are Connaught Circle competition for Starbucks, yet here it is, an ultramodern building with plate-glass windows, armchairs that softly cradle a biker's buttocks, chocolate ice cream, brownies, and perfect espresso pulled from a real chrome and brass Italian espresso machine. We three are the only customers.

We linger overlong and dusk is falling as we ride into Jaipur. Francis consults his *Lonely Planet* for accommodation. A biker pulls alongside. Are we looking for a guest house? Very cheap, very clean. Not in guidebook.

Hindu or Muslim?

A moment's pause before he admits to Muslim.

Muslims are less caste-ridden. And not in a guidebook so not packed with our fellow foreigners. We may even meet Indians.

We have hit gold. The guest house that is not in any guidebook is down a reasonably quiet side street in the city centre. The lobby leads to a small central garden. Rooms are on the first floor, small but clean and with clean bathrooms. My only complaint is the hardness of the mattresses. Best is a restaurant on the ground floor that doesn't function so I feel no guilt or embarrassment at eating elsewhere.

Francis was too adventurous yesterday. Dysentery has felled him. He lies in bed for the next three days. Miyuki nurses both him and her head cold. Meanwhile Jaipur is a delight to explore, The old city is a maze of narrow lanes, artisans in tiny open-doored workshops, vast bazaars, museums, palaces, great merchants' houses. Dawn is the best hour, streets near empty. A cook makes delicious omelettes at a stall just inside the main gate to the walled city. Even the coffee is good. Read the *Times* or the *Hindu*. Watch the city awake as the rising sun brings a soft glow to the pink walls of the palaces and *havelis*. Perfect start to a day...

I am due back in Jaipur in a couple of weeks for the literary festival. The festival site is a slightly run-down palace, now a hotel, outside the old city walls, big garden and a pretty courtyard. The restaurant is beyond my budget. I've found an open-fronted Punjabi place with a traditional clay tanduri oven. Chickens are small and skinny as a Paris model, great taste and definitely free range.

Meanwhile I have a monthly column to write for British Airways. The owner of our guest house is large, friendly, conversational and helpful. A table is set in the garden and he finds an extension lead for my laptop. A young boy who should be at school fetches tea or fresh lemon soda from a neighbouring stall. Miyuki sits with me in the sun for a while. Her head cold is easing and Francis is on the mend. We can ride on to Pushkar in the morning...

Jaipur to Pushkar is 150 kilometres due west. We should leave at dawn. Francis has graduated from his Egyptian sojourn with a first in unpunctuality. I sit in the lobby and watch cricket on television.

The guest house owner is one more Muhammed. He sends out for coffee and we watch a bowler whose name I don't know bowl a wide and a no ball in the same over.

'Very bad,' judges Muhammed.

The bowler's captain obviously agrees.

Muhammed's eldest son is a cricketer, bowling and batting. 'Very good,' Muhammed assures me. The boy is 14 years old and plays in his high school eleven and has played once in his age group for Rajasthan.

I ask what sort of school. Catholic and private. 'Very expensive,' Muhammed says. I convert rupees to pounds: £60 a term, £180 for the year.

Youth cricket interests me. I was fixture secretary for Herefordshire and managed the under 16s. Muhammed writes in the reservation diary the date for my return for the literary festival and promises to keep me the big corner room. 'Very comfortable,' he says. And if I have time, I can watch his son practise at the sports club.

Splendid.

Miyuki appears somewhat shamefaced. Francis is nearly packed. 'Fifteen minutes,' she promises.

For 15 read 30.

Francis is in the lead. He has chosen a short cut. The short cut is not a highway. It is two-lane tar with dirt detours and a fine collection of holidaying heavy machinery, mostly yellow. Long queues of overladen trucks rock and grind from deep pothole to deep pothole. Air is 80 per cent diesel fumes. Indian towns are in permanent rush hour; we navigate two. Both Francis and Miyuki wear face scarves. I have a clinician's nose and mouth mask on thin elastic that snaps when I take my helmet off. I should enjoy snapping Francis's neck. I am trying not to hate India and I would betray all that I hold sacred for sight of a CaféDay.

The road to Pushkar branches off the non-highway a few miles short of Ajmer. The road leads up over steep hills and is good tar with few vehicles. The air is fresh. Happiness renewed, I zip past Francis and pull in at the top of the ascent. Pushkar lies below. The guidebook reports a pilgrimage city with temples encircling a central lake. Lakes are sun-sparkling water. There is no sparkle. The road down is a fun series of S bends, delightful biking. We take a sharp left at the bus stop down a dirt lane and take the left fork where the lane splits. The Pushkar Palace Guest House is a two-level concrete dormitory block overlooking a large frangipani-perfumed garden of dry uncut grass, shrubs, a few palm trees. Six foreigners and three locals are building a fire in the centre of a circle of semi-usable garden chairs and a couple of cement benches. A large roll-up changes hands and the air is thick with the scent of marijuana. The roll-up explains the extreme slowness of the fire-building. The kitchen and office shack to the left of the gates are unattended.

A young local in vest, wrap-round and flip flops abandons the fire-building to sign us in. The price is good and the local carries my bag upstairs to a pleasant room with a clean bathroom and views across fields to the hills. Exhausted by carrying the bag, the local collapses on to the bed and produces the makings for a fresh roll-up from a cotton pouch. I suggest he visits Francis and Miyuki. He says, OK, but that the boiler is broken. His logic is pleasing: good dope will make either the cold water bearable or make me forgo having a shower. No dope, so he promises to send up a bucket of hot water. The hot water is a mirage. The cold water is bearable, just.

The fire burns brightly in the garden. I find Francis comparing Enfield mechanical mishaps with two stoned Norwegian bikers. The guest house cook is semi-comatose in a deckchair. The Norwegians report that he does breakfast, sometimes lunch. Evening times he is too stoned. There is a good restaurant at the junction of the two lanes…

Francis has researched Pushkar on the internet. Pushkar's sacred lake dropped to earth from the divine hands of Brahma. Temples surround the lake and good Hindus are obligated to make at least one pilgrimage to shrive their sins in the holy water. Travellers report that watching the sun set over the water is a life-changing experience. We discover that a politician, anxious for votes, has had the lake cleaned. The cleaning pierced the clay seal. The lake no longer holds water and the 50 or more holy ghats lead down to dry mud and a tiny central puddle. Ah, well…

A cold beer would be good after visiting three temples. However alcohol is forbidden within the sacred city's limits, so are eggs and meat. We make do with chilled lime and soda at an outdoor ice cream parlour on the central square. A dozen skeletal Westerners of both sexes, great age, long hair and big-bead necklaces occupy the next table. They have drifted through decades of hallucinatory visions. Now all-knowing, nothing surprises them. Their conversation is sweet smiles and gentle nods interspersed with the occasional monosyllable. A chocolate ice cream cornet, God, marijuana and the universe are interchangeable.

The restaurant at the junction of the two lanes serves excellent vegetarian food in a garden sheltered by high walls. Back at the guest house, the two Norwegian bikers have been joined by a third, also with an ancient Enfield. Francis is in heaven. Miyuki goes to bed. I talk with a young couple from Arizona who have been seeking salvation at a yoga centre in Rishikesh, Himalaya home of the Dalai Lama. Lack of central heating has driven them south. Pushkar is fun and I love India. So to sleep…

A fresh sunlit morning and Francis and Miyuki are still abed. I ride in search of a better breakfast than that promised by the Pushkar Palace's stoned cook. A young man with ginger dreadlocks sits on the steps of a guest house further down the lane. He points at me and says, 'Simon Gandolfi…'

I, super cool, say, 'Hi.'

Such is fame…

Or writing of my travels for the *Guardian*.

The Pushkar Palace Guest House is Enfield Central; four more bikers are in residence. One of the new arrivals is an American fire-eater. She is a small, vital woman, not an ounce of fat. Eagle feathers lance upright from greying hair dragged back above ears decorated with hummingbird feathers – silver nose studs, lots of wrist bangles and lots of rings, one of which is a silver skull. She rides a cut-down Bullet 500 and is on her way south to Goa. The other bikers are here to celebrate her birthday and to bid farewell to the eldest of the Norwegians. This Norwegian is equally grey, equally vital and equally fat free; dress is heavy black biker boots, faded Levis gone at the knees, a sleeveless white undershirt beneath a chrome-studded leather waistcoat and wall-to-wall tattoos. His bike has a custom seat with a padded back that rises head high and is decorated with a fine array of bronze Hindu gods. He has been biking round India for 10 years. An extension to his present visa has been refused and he is advised that no further visa will be issued. He hasn't the money for an airline ticket so the Norwegian Embassy will have to fly him home. I wonder what income has supported him during his Indian sojourn. Asking would be impolite.

Pushkar is definitely fun. I am in love with the diminutive fire-eater. We Brits are seldom incurious. We are merely shy of touching on that which we consider intimate. As for instance, how much of the decoration does the birthday girl wear in bed? Obviously not the feathers – unless she has an unlimited supply. And surely some of the silverware would catch in the sheets. And how does she rid her breath of the petrol smell after a performance. There was a time when I might have found out…

I do ask where she performs. Ferociously expensive Delhi and Goa weddings of India's new rich. Having an American woman perform reinforces their self-worth – this is the birthday girl's explanation, and that the bride's parents enjoy boasting of the wedding's cost.

Miyuki and Francis are exploring. I have a clip and beard-trim at a one-chair barber's shop two metres wide by three deep right beside the garden restaurant. The barber is my age. Were he plumper, he would have to find new premises. A young silversmith has a shop the other side of the restaurant. He and the barber are in cahoots. The barber soaps my face, shaves one cheek; his mobile buzzes.

'Being sorry,' he says and steps outside. Next moment the silversmith is proffering a wooden tray of silver trinkets and lapis lazuli. I am trapped beneath a reasonably clean towel. The barber has a cutthroat razor. I do not expect him to cut my throat. However, I am nervous. Mostly of his not sharpening the razor. And I don't wish to be rude, particularly as we must pass the silversmith's shop each time we go to the restaurant.

Pushkar is known for its silversmiths and this young man's work is good. I carry a bronze medallion of the Angel of Hope, farewell gift from my brother and sister-in-law. The silversmith will mount the medallion in silver and make a chain. The negotiations take a while. Soap dries on my face. Fresh lather and a fresh blade.

Another splendid day in Pushkar: temples, ice cream and updating my diary. The medallion is mounted, the chain made. I have paid the silversmith. He has splurged the medallion money on dope. Miyuki, Francis and I head for the garden restaurant for a late supper. The entire staff are comatose beneath the corner awning. We go elsewhere.

Our last night at the Pushkar Palace Guest House. Diet has been vegetarian in this holy city. The restaurateur has invited us to dine sinfully at his home. He rides a scooter. We follow down dirt tracks bordering fields and across narrow wooden bridges that span dry drainage ditches. Cows are transformed into massive monsters by a mid-sized moon and stars brilliant in a night sky free of industrial pollution. The *phut phut* of irrigation sprinklers heralds a drop in temperature; in this dry land, damp earth and fresh growth has a rich thick scent. A goat bleats as we pull in to the courtyard of a square concrete-block farmhouse where we sit cross-legged on bare tiles. The restaurateur has brought a dozen bottles of lager in a freezer bag. The air becomes thick and pungent as roll-ups circulate. Female hands proffer big aluminium bowls to our host through the part-opened door: jointed chickens, chunks of tough mutton, brindles, potato, cauliflower, all in thick heavily spiced sauces. This is true Rajasthan peasant food, deliciously yummy and very different from the more sophisticated vegetarian fare served at the restaurant. A small son sits on his father's lap. Dad feeds him titbits. No daughters – daughters don't count. Conversation slows, bellies distend. I long for bed. Secondary smoke has affected my balance. Or maybe age is responsible. I kneel with hands on the wall and crawl my way up. A slight stumble brings a giggle from Miyuki.

Francis asks if I'm OK to ride.

Fresh air and I'll be fine but keep the speed down…

Fifteen years prior to today's ride west from Pushkar, a senior police officer raped a teenage tennis player. The girl's family demanded justice. The police persecuted the girl's family, frequently arresting her brother on trumped-up charges. The girl committed suicide. The police chief was promoted. Now, finally, the High Court has sentenced the police chief to five years in prison. Police have refused to arrest him. A local politician has protested by sitting on the railway line and blocking the slow express. In their hunt for the politician, police have blocked the highway to Jodhpur. Francis, Miyuki and I have six lanes of good tar to ourselves. How does it feel? A little weird! Equally weird will be my change of ambience. I have been invited to spend two nights at the Taj Hotel's Umaid Bhawan Palace.

I am familiar with the history of the Umaid Bhawan Palace. I know that it has 347 rooms and that it was built in the years 1933 to 1937 at the command of His Highness Raj Rajeshwar Saramad-i-Rajha-i-Hindustan Maharajadhiraja Maharajah Shri Sir Umaid Singh Sahib Bahadur, Maharajah of Jodhpur, Knight Grand Commander of the Order of the Star of India, Knight Grand Commander of the

Order of the Indian Empire, Knight Commander of the Royal Victorian Order. I know that construction coincided with a seven-year drought, that Rajasthan's farmers and their families were starving and that His Highness the Maharajah ordered construction to give the peasantry work. His Highness already owned various palaces. The Umaid Bhawan Palace was strictly a charity project. A seven-mile railway connected the sandstone quarries to the building site. No cement was used in the construction. Each immense sandstone block was carved and lowered by crane on to a block of ice. The ice enabled workers to manoeuvre the blocks into exact position. An ice factory in a time of drought? Workers who were peasant farmers. Ah well....

The palace sits on a hill overlooking the town of Jodhpur. It is the only building on the hill. Two sentries guard the driveway. A call is made to the palace. The barrier is lifted. The driveway leads to a sweep of gravel sized for military parades. A doorman in elaborate fancy dress and a mammoth moustache commands an entrance portico designed for elephant-drawn carriages – large elephants. The doorman has a master's degree in the exacting science of door-opening. His bows offer an infallible guide to guests' social standing.

Small motorcycles don't have doors.

Fat old men on small motorcycles don't have social standing.

The situation is saved by the young front desk manager. He has doctorates both in charm and in manners. Busboys untie the suitcase and small backpack; panniers are unloaded into cotton laundry bags; a serf in gardener's garb rides the bike away. The front desk manager conducts me to my room. We are followed by a small procession. In the lead is a waiter carrying a chilled lime and soda on a silver tray. A bath is suggested as a preparation to signing the guest register. All this is done without the slightest hint that I am odd.

As to the room, it is comfortable. It is not grand. It is not romantic. It does not compare with a suite at the Taj Usha Kiran Palace in Gwalior nor does it possess the charm of Orchha's Bundelkhand Riverside. Modern five-star hotel functional seems an accurate description, though European in size rather than North American, lots of marble, lots of lights, crisp bed linen, delicious scents and soaps in the bathroom, fresh fruit, fresh flowers. So, no, no complaints. However, I do suspect that it is the smallest room in the hotel section of the palace. A room for impecunious relations – such is the just desserts for a writer whose travels are chronicled in the decidedly socialist *Guardian* rather than the *Wall Street Journal*. And the furniture is familiar, the desk, chairs – even the light fittings. You will find them in any illustration of the art deco period. Maples of Oxford Street made the originals. A German submarine torpedoed the ship en route to Bombay; these are Indian-made to the original designs.

I am comped for bed and breakfast. Not for dinner. I am bathed, changed into clean clothes and hungry. My bike has gone. Too far to walk into town, too far to a restaurant in my price bracket. The hotel's dining room is art deco glory with windows facing out over lawns and a lake-sized infinity pool. Below (where they should be) twinkle the lights of the town.

The maître d'hôtel conducts me to a corner table at the rear of the dining room. Waiters hover while I study the menu. Cheapest entrée is a curry of lambs liver (barely twice the price of a night in a *Lonely Planet* guest house). Negative on the wine, thank you, plain water will do nicely…

A table of determinedly confident and noisy Indians adorned with gold bullion sit at a table up front. Some way to their left, also up front, sit an Indian couple, young and possibly on their honeymoon. Up front my end of the dining room sit an Australian husband and wife. Thirteen guests in a dining room staffed to seat a hundred and this is peak season – such is the aftermath of the terrorist attack on the Bombay Taj. Rich tourists stay away…

Bedtime in a Taj Palace hotel is sybaritic. The room steward has folded away the counterpane, turned down the top sheet. A fresh frangipani flower nestles on my pillow. Baby rose petals scent the towels. Deliciously crisp bed linen is an invitation to bare-skin snuggling and the mattress is perfect.

Breakfast is comped. I must eat sufficient to last till supper. A sedate swim up and down the infinity pool encourages appetite and breakfast is magnificent. A sort of inverse racism amongst young Europeans claims that this luxury is for foreigners. That it is not the real India. The true India is poverty-stricken; lives in a mud and wattle hut; a male who beats his wife; a wife who grinds her own flour and cooks outdoors over a wood fire.

Yet most guests at the Umaid Bhawan Palace are Indian and most guests at the Usha Kiran Palace were Indian.

I am conducted on a tour of the palace. We climb marble stairs to the suites originally designed for visiting Maharajahs and Maharanis. Tiger skins on the walls of a small courtyard are an assault on the animal lover. Second thought: black stripes on a gold background, how brilliantly art deco. A three-tier glass fountain rises from a small pool. Flowers float in each of the three bowls; frangipani, rose petals and bougainvillea. Each suite gives entry to a fantasy world of marble, carved wood, Persian prayer rugs and embroidered hangings; beds are emperor-size and raised high so that royalty may sleep closer to God.

Rising at the head of the Maharajah's bed is mirrored glass in a gold frame. Imagine the Maharajah, naturally on top, checking the waxed points of his moustaches.

But, oh, the Maharanis. At the bed head is a near life-size painting on glass depicting a blond 1920s flapper astride a leaping tiger. Take one look at her face, diaphanous shorty nightdress, arms flung high – this is a chick who has just hit, really hit. A pure splendid wow of total exultation!

'The god Kali,' says my young guide.

'The what?' I say. 'Have you ever looked? Really looked?'

He steps back. A long pause. Then, 'No…'

Yes. Absolutely yes…

And inlaid into the Maharani's dressing table is a bull under the whip plunging out of the water. Surely, *Give it to me or else...*

Though built in the twenties, this is the India of Victorian imagination.

Oh to be super rich for a single night.

There is more of course, so many delights: for the Maharajah's ladies, an indoor pool, surrounds mosaicked with the signs of the Zodiac. But why list them all? If you can, go visit. Here were two British architects let loose on an unlimited budget. They were having fun.

'Hey, what about a squash court?'

'Why not two?'

'Marble?'

'Absolutely...'

Prior to the Umaid Bhawan Palace, Jodphur's Maharajah made do with a palace within the hilltop fortress that dominates the town. The fortress is almost indistinguishable at a distance from the sheer-sided rock that crowns the hill. A rickshaw driver asks for 100 rupees to run me up the hill. We settle for 40. The narrow twisting lane through town is surfaced with craters and divided by open drains and speed bumps. Why speed bumps when a Ducati under maximum acceleration might make 15 kph before the next bend or the next hole in the road? That is without the hindrance of cows, rickshaws, motorbikes, bicycles, pushcarts, absent-minded pedestrians and kids playing tag. As a charity project, a sewage system might have been more beneficial than a palace

Sunday and a never-ending river of visitors flows from the ticket office. My fellow oldies stumble upward. Watch their eyes as they measure how much further they must climb, questioning whether they can make it; comprehending now the ambulance on standby below the gate in the outer ramparts. All have guidebooks in hand, camera at the ready. The flow weakens on the outside of a sharp hairpin above the second gate. I break clear and turn downhill towards a lesser palace nestling within the outer walls. The shade of a lime tree transforms a low parapet into perfect seating.

To my right a bunch of donkeys, empty sacks across their saddles, wait placidly beside a pile of builder's sand. All the donkeys but one are small and grey. The exception is white, larger and older than the others. He keeps to the shade of a tree while a labourer loads the other mokes with sand. Last to be loaded, he intends to be unloaded first and heads immediately down a steep dirt path with the others following.

Swim along a coral reef and you will see the big fish and the big coral. Stay still, the more you notice. Detail by smaller detail emerges. Travelling is the same. I have been seated here on the parapet beneath this tree for close on two hours. Enough sun filters through the leaves to keep me pleasantly warm. Mostly I have been looking upward. The fortress appears to be a continuation of the precipice from which it grows, rock on rock, up and up, the highest levels honeycombed with decorative caves and balconies and topped with a filigreed crown of marble. The sky beyond the fortress is a clear royal blue of extraordinary depth. Tilting my head centres the sky and the fortress through an old stone arch and over a newish building of golden sandstone. The contrast between golden sandstone, grey rock and sky is of a beauty to be enjoyed and enjoyed and be blown away by. Who needs psychedelics? And why move until the sun sets? Travelling in company, such blissful peace is hard to come by.

Matchstick tourists look down from the fortress balconies. They look out across the town and beyond the outer fortifications to a ravaged land of rock quarries. The sky there on the horizon is sun-bleached. I look back up at the deep blue backdrop to the fortress. Doves have occupied every available hole on the rock face and in the fortress walls. They coo softly. Gliding off the fortress, their arched wings have the rigidity of plastic models. Three green parakeets have begun an argument in my tree – or perhaps discussion is more accurate; they don't sound cross.

Imagine a foot soldier in an attacking army advancing out of the desert. Mehrangarh Fortress is an island rock soaring vertically out of the dust cloud that shrouds the attack. Dust is in the soldier's throat and in his eyes and encrusts his nostrils. Water is short. Food is almost non-existent. Already exhausted, he must storm fortification after fortification merely to reach the foot of the precipice above which soar the fortress walls. Please God, no, not this...

India and Pakistan loathe each other. They have been either heading for war or at war ever since partition. India suspects the Pakistan army of attempting a blitzkrieg across the Tsar desert. Jaisalmer is at the desert's edge. The road west from Jodphur to Jaisalmer is wide two-lane tar in excellent condition. It is a military road and maintained by the military.

I am back with Francis and Miyuki. We ride across a flat land of small villages surrounded by a few irrigated fields; and dry fields of thin soil ready-ploughed but barren without rain and vulnerable to the desert winds. The fields beyond the village environs give way to sand, sparse scrub and thorn trees. Francis leads the way. He has zero confidence in his Enfield's engine and keeps to a steady 35 miles an hour. I have total confidence in my little Honda. The road is empty and 35 is too slow. And there are memories here in the acacias and trains of burdened camels that plod the road edge; memories of Africa and of my youth that I would plunder were I free. Not a car or truck in sight and I speed past a smiling Miyuki and slalom the white lines.

We stop three times in villages for bottled water and for the Enfield's engine to cool. A journey that should take four hours takes six. Finally the sandstone battlements of the walled city float above the horizon. Irrigation sprinklers spin on fields of young wheat. The fields give way to a low-level wave of concrete sprawl that grows and breaks below sandstone battlements that rise golden in the evening sun.

The road leads up to great gates and on up to the square where broad steps mount to the palace complex from where, in olden days,

the Maharajah controlled the desert road and exacted taxes on cara-
vans. The present Maharajah inhabits a new-build set in gardens out
by the ancient artificial lake that once supplied the town with water.

Within the battlements, the intricately carved facades of Jain
temples and fine *havelis* line the narrow streets. Control of the desert
road made Jaisalmer's merchants rich. Those glory days are gone.
Modern Jaisalmer competes with Pushkar as a backpacker's haven.
Scruffy guest houses are its attraction, tea houses, bottom-end restaurants, cheap dope and tourist pimps.

We find rooms with ornate ceilings in a *haveli* that has seen better
days, carpets threadbare and lighting barely adequate. Charm is in
the panelling and antique beds. Counterpanes are embroidered and
blankets thick; very necessary in chill desert nights. Days are perfect
for exploring, warm with clear skies, sun imparting a soft glow to the
town's golden sandstone.

We have discovered hope for Francis's Enfield. Two Sikh brothers
work their magic in a minute workshop directly below the battlements. No room for a workbench, the brothers squat on the floor,
tools strewn left and right. They are rebuilding the engine of a 1950s
350. Battered hubcaps hold engine parts. Petrol in the hubcaps
is black with old oil and carbon; a pedestal fan fights the fumes
without noticeable success.

Francis parks beside a shiny new Bullet 500 with a sheet of black
plastic wrapped over its engine where the head should be. A 350 is
missing a rear wheel assembly. And there is one skeleton without
wheels. Francis's bike looks what it is; old, tattered, tired. We wait
while the elder Sikh brother finishes whatever he is doing in the
workshop. He eyes Francis's bike with a minimum of enthusiasm,
starts the engine, listens, revs, nods to himself, swings into the
saddle, rides off down the dirt lane below the battlements, does a
U-turn and returns. The brakes squeak as he draws up. A further nod
is in agreement with his initial disapproval. He taps a number into a
mobile, talks and hands the mobile to Francis. The Sikh's wife is on

the other end. She speaks good English and will come to translate once her office closes.

We are stuck in Jaisalmer for four days. The engine on Francis's bike is in pieces. So is the gearbox. There has been much nodding during the disassembly, much pointing to this and that. Final conclusion waits on the elder brother's wife to translate. She is a business gradu- ate and occupies a government office eight hours a day. An indeter- minate number of indeterminate relatives share a modern house in the suburbs. Various bits of engine hide beneath beds and benches and the house smells of petrol. We have been invited to dinner – vegetarian, simple and lightly spiced. What and how we eat is of great interest. Everyone watches. Everyone smiles. Various women pass babies one to another. All conversation must go via the wife so comes to a halt each time she goes to the kitchen.

We learn that her husband has developed various modifications for Enfields. What modifications is a mystery as the wife is no mechanic and her vocabulary is inadequate – however bikers ride even from Jodhpur to have their Enfields improved. Francis's bike is beyond improvement without a complete rebuild. It has been badly modi- fied by a mechanic without understanding and the rebuild would take weeks as the parts must come from the factory in Chennai. Elder brother is returning the bike to normal and readjusting carbu- rettor and timing. Francis should ride it slowly.

Jaisalmer glowing in the evening sun is glorious. A multitude of fis- sures and holes in the sandstone battlements are perfect nest shelter. Doves wheel and dive, breaking at the last instant to alight. Squirrels scamper across a small courtyard. These are the palm squirrels with three stripes up their backs that are common in India: *funambulus palmarum*. Home in Herefordshire, grey squirrels live in the giant cedar shading the lawn outside our kitchen. Greys are immigrants from the US; they murder our smaller indigenous reds. Would Brits have noticed an invasion of the American red squirrel? And had they been pale-skinned, would immigrants from Africa or Asia have aroused less antipathy amongst conservative Brits? Squirrels are of the family *Sciuridae*. We are *Homo sapiens*. Pondering on squirrels is an effective break on my desire to hold Miyuki's hand.

I have had a camel-skin bag tailored to fit across the Honda's pillion seat. Francis has decided on a major rebuild of his Enfield. He and Miyuki are off to the desert on a camel safari. Desert for me is sand in the food and being shot at. I have watched the Sikh brother rebuild the 1950s 350, watched as elder brother primed the carburettor. His confidence is palpable. One preparatory kick, then hard, and an immediate *brrmm* as he opens the throttle. He squats to adjust the idle. The engine burbles happily. He looks up at me over the saddle and smiles. A biker in search of mechanical romance should order a rebuilt Bullet from the brothers (Gvinder Kour at Punjab Motors is on Facebook). Take the train from Jodphur to Jaisalmer. Then true biker bliss…

Meanwhile I must return to Jaipur for the literary festival.

5

RETURN TO JAIPUR

I am a lone traveller urinating at the roadside midway between Jaisalmer and Jodhpur. Two gazelles eye me from the shade of an acacia tree. The tree draws thin shadow patterns through loose scrub. Wind shifts the surface sand in small eddies up a low ridge. The gazelles turn and trot off over the ridge. Down the highway a camel curls its upper lip back as it nibbles shoots from a thorn tree. I remount the Honda, press the button and the engine purrs. I am beholden to nobody, have no set route. What blissful contentment.

I have taken a roundabout route not on the road atlas. Straight country roads divide flat farmland into squares. Roads are single lane, long stretches of good tar alternating with graded dirt and with steeplechase courses of ruts and potholes. Fields are green, music the swish and phut of irrigation sprinklers, a woman calling a child. The road narrows through small market towns. Loaded donkeys and trucks with bald tyres edge between high whitewashed walls. The few windows are minute. An open doorway gives a glimpse of a courtyard, women hunkered on their haunches, clay stove, big-bellied water pots.

Food is dal and thick fresh yoghurt, sliced onion and a few peeled tomatoes that I wash in bottled water. Bed is a string stretcher under a neem tree outside a village café. Barefoot children watch as village men attempt a conversation that is mostly hand signs. Sometimes a village schoolteacher will attempt a few sentences. This is the India of my memories rediscovered. A backpacker's marijuana-scented night in Pushkar keeps memories alight. So on to Jaipur and a corner room in the Muslim-owned guest house.

Three Bombay academics are my companions at the Jaipur Literary Festival. These are big women, very sure of themselves and confident in their opinions. I mention Mumbai.

'Bombay,' they correct. 'Mumbai is for foreign newscasters...'

They refer to the festival as the William Dalrymple Self Glorification Festival. They don't like him. And he is all-pervasive – even interrupting an evening concert with a reading from his latest book. This is too much for Bombay's Intellectual Amazons. Three large women barging their way through rows of packed chairs is a riot.

In defence of William Dalrymple, I have read his books. All of them. Even the new one. My favourite, *From the Holy Mountain*. He has reason to be proud. My agent gave me an introduction (he is on first-name terms with everyone). I emailed William Dalrymple from London my awareness that he would be busy in the lead-up to the festival. William Dalrymple emailed back suggesting we have a drink in Jaipur. I introduce myself. He turns his back on me.

Dalrymple shares a platform the following day with the founder of the *Lonely Planet* empire, Tony Wheeler. *The Best of Travel* is the most recent *Lonely Planet* anthology. I am one of the contributing authors. Tony Wheeler has written the foreword. I introduce myself. Tony Wheeler turns his back on me.

Three young Nigerian writers interview me. Why me? God knows.

We talk of Africa. Time I return, they say, rediscover my love for the continent. Why not celebrate my seventy-eighth birthday in Lagos? They will put me up at a boutique hotel, arrange a ride with the local biker club, disport myself on the dance floor, experiment with a new drink or two, give a few readings, a few interviews. Finally a few days' recuperation out on the beach. No politics. Strictly fun – fun is something I can hack.

A mini tribe of black-skinned Untouchables camps on the pavement of a street down which I ride each morning. Small children are naked, none have shoes. Female hairstyle is a tangled matt. Where do they wash? Defecate?

I am seated next to a fair-skinned Brahman lady. I mention the Untouchables.

'Those people, they won't work,' she says. 'They enjoy living like that.'

The owner of the guest house has invited me to dinner at his home in the old city. He, his sons and I sit on the floor. Food is a rich mutton biryani, chicken, bowls of okra and cauliflower. My host takes me up on to the roof to admire the view over the town. We have to pass through the kitchen, which is the women's zone. His wife is furious.

The guest house owner's eldest son is a large lad, 14 years old and a cricketer. He has played in his age group for Rajasthan. I am to watch him at practice at the sports club. The boy returns from school. His father hands him a helmet and the keys to his bike. I ride pillion all the way across town. The boy stops at red lights, looks left and right at intersections. His mobile buzzes, he doesn't answer. Unbelievable. And what a cricketer. He bowls fast and straight, never a loose ball, and his batting is fearless with fluent leg drives and off – this against bowlers older by three and four years.

That he was dropped from the Rajasthan team seems inexplicable.

'What caste are you,' I ask his father.

'Mutton killer,' he confesses.

'That's pretty low,' say I.

'About as low as you can get,' says the father.

'I thought Muslims didn't believe in castes,' say I.

'Yes, but we are being Hindu Muslims,' says the father with a waggle of his head.

And the boy attends a Catholic school. Such is India…

6

SOUTH TO GOA

Jaipur south to Bundi is a 220-kilometre doddle across flat farmland on a good road. Indian Bundi is an industrial city. Tourist Bundi is a thin strip of seventeenth- and eighteenth-century *havelis* converted into hotels and guest houses with rooftop restaurants. For tourists the attractions are the thirteenth-century fort and decaying palace. Both *Footprint* and *Lonely Planet* recommend Lake View Paying Guest House. The lake in question is a square tank half full with green scum.

A kindly Austrian Buddhist hikes my camel bag up three flights of steep stone stairs and across the flat roof to my 400-rupee room. I follow slowly with backpack and helmet and collapse on a king-size bed. Survive the climb and the room is heaven – sofa, easy chair and upholstered lolling space beneath arched windows that filter sunlight through stained glass. Murals of painted flowers and garden greenery surround the windows. The ceiling border is gold and blue. A mural of a smiling young woman livens the wall beside the bathroom door. So the bathroom is basic – big deal.

I share a stone bench on the terrace with the Austrian Buddhist and gaze with joy across the rooftops at the palace cascading down the hillside. Ancient walls glow in the misty evening sunlight – so does the herbal cigarette the Buddhist offers. I decline politely and wonder that a Buddhist dope-smoker should earn his bread as a technical engineer at a Swiss nuclear power station. Easy there, don't panic but do remember to say your prayers.

The roof is a way station for monkeys on their evening trek home to the fort. One picks up a torn black T-shirt from the parapet and shakes it aloft. The shirt envelops his head. Blinded, he chatters with fear and tears at the cotton. The shirt catches on a water pipe and drags loose. Off he scampers. I go in search of a shave and dinner.

Out of bed at 7 a.m. A lovely room and sad that I must leave so early. The Buddhist nuclear engineer is meditating. Eyes closed, he sits facing the morning sun in the lotus position. A josh stick has replaced the herbal. I pack and hump my backpack and bag downstairs, load the bike, then return to an upper courtyard in search of a bill. The owner is a small kindly man of my generation. The *haveli* was built by his great-grandfather, prime minister of the state in the days of the Maharajahs. Family members help in running the guest house. There is so much that could be done to improve the place: fix the lavatory cistern in my room, freshen paintwork, tidy the lakeside garden – simple tasks that, were this our home, Bernadette and I would enjoy. The owners are the wrong caste. They don't do manual and they can't afford help; the lovely building crumbles.

I ride a short way to a café in search of breakfast. A male toddler in a yellow bed cap tied under the chin, no pants, points at me. I point back. He giggles coyly. His dad sweeps him up and tells him to shake my hand. He whimpers. His mum grabs him and ducks back through a low doorway. The teenage help at the café says that there is no coffee and no tea and no fresh orange juice because there is no electricity. Electric orange juice?

A bearded Muslim grandfather in a white skullcap, knee-length white shirt and loose white cotton trousers rides four children to infants' school on an ancient Honda 125 – three on the pillion, one straddling the gas tank. I follow in his wake. Farewell to Bundi.

A minor road runs south-west through dark emerald wheat fields and small villages. The oncoming traffic is mostly bikers delivering milk to town – presumably to a dairy to be transformed into cheese and curd. Four churns is the standard load. Some men manage six. The churns are copper and bell-bottomed.

Here, way off the highway, riding through villages demands extra caution. The tarmac is already sun-warmed and the street is extra living space. A cow dozes in the sun; a woman combs out her hair; men gather round a spectacled reader of a newspaper. Men and women are dressed in Sunday best. The only people working are the milk deliverymen and bus drivers. Today must be one more of India's innumerable holidays.

An egret pretends to be a heron on the borders of a shallow reed-rimmed lake. The road zigzags up and crosses a barren plateau cratered with stone quarries, then down to more wheat fields and finally meets the four-lane Highway 76. The highway is almost deserted. The concrete surface is excellent and the Honda cruises happily at 90 kph (yes, I'm a real speed freak). I overtake four men on two bikes riding side by side. All four are speaking into their mobiles while speaking to each other.

The turn south to Dhariyawad is 100 kilometres of dilatory meandering on single-track tar. Men have gathered in every village. Serious-faced, they squat and talk quietly in the shade of flat-topped acacia, neem or mango trees, few women visible.

Shops are shuttered as I ride through the narrow main street of Dhariyawad's bazaar. I have ridden 368 kilometres. My butt is numb but what a totally joyous day.

Dhariyawad is an Indian country market town at the confluence of the Jakham and Karmoi rivers. There is no logical reason for visiting Dhariyawad. The route I took from Bundi is a long way round. The easiest approach is from Udaipur east on National Highway 79 to Bhatewar. A single-track road leads south from Bhatewar for 50 kilometres. The road is bad tar with crumbling edges – not a comforting drive for the nervous. The road passes through teak forest. Teak, when shedding its leaves, looks more dead than alive. The forest is a wildlife sanctuary. Langur monkeys are common – as they are elsewhere. The fortunate may spot four-horned antelope, nilgai, possibly a jackal or hyena. The miraculously fortunate (or imaginative) may even spot a panther stalk the shadows, though I doubt that even the evening flight of giant flying squirrels warrants the drive. So let me offer a very different experience: a rest from sightseeing, escape from the tourist route. No *havelis* here tarted up as guest houses, no restaurants promising veg and non-veg, Chinese, Italian, continental (all tasting much the same), no tiresome tourist touts.

Drive through the market and through the bazaar. At the T-junction turn right through the pointed keyhole archway emblazoned with a radiant sun smiling over a Rajput moustache – the massive wooden doors should be open – and you enter a sixteenth-century mini paradise centred on a late nineteenth-century mansion converted into a Heritage Hotel: the Dhariyawad Fort. This is the domain of the eldest living son of the eldest son of the Jagirdar of Dhariyawad. The 16 spacious rooms and suites offer total peace, comfortable beds, comfortable easy chairs and always a desk. Bathrooms are huge, water hot, proper towels.

The future Jagirdar of Dhariyawad is also president of the local branch of Congress, India's ruling and dominant political party. I have arrived on election day for mayors and district assemblies – the village gatherings are explained. The Jagirdar has been out marshalling his men (no women) to get the vote in; a moment to greet me with great politeness, then back to oversee the count.

I am the only guest. My ground-floor room opens off the front terrace where an elderly retainer serves dinner. A full moon softly lights the gardens. What could be more romantic?

Only at breakfast do I realise why I feel so at home. The Fort has the feel of a small manor house in an English village or off a cathedral close, though too small to be a bishop's palace. Arches are a different shape, servants more numerous, home-made marmalade marginally less chunky. But the feel is there: peaceful, unpretentious, timeless, embedded in the community. What joy to be able to stay a month, ride horseback, bird-watch, explore tribal villages, wander the bazaar without being nagged with *buy buy buy*. Yes, and tell tall tales later of the panther seen while following a forest guide…

Sunrise in Dhariyawad. The Congress Party has swept the board.

The spoils must be divided – small groups of male activists gather on the lawn below the hotel terrace. I watch the Jagirdar mingle, affable, contented. Seeking greater privacy, a couple drift away; the elder gives instructions; the younger nods.

Victory music blares from loudspeakers in the bazaar. Later starts the victory procession. The Jagirdar leads in his jeep. Small hatchbacks follow, motorcyclists two abreast. A tight group of women in sari glad rags smile respectful support from beyond the archway – so much for equality of the sexes. The procession moves away through the bazaar and market square. The music fades.

The Jagirdar's majordomo accompanies me in search of an ATM. He murmurs greetings left and right – a semi-semi royal progress. I follow in his footsteps – traditionally the woman's place. The ATM won't pay. Bloody hell… Back to the Fort and back to work.

Drum and firecrackers herald Congress footsoldiers' return through the bazaar. The brave spill through the archway into the Fort's parking lot. A fresh firecracker volley and roll of drums encourages the timid. They have come to pay homage only to find the Jagirdar absent. More firecrackers, more rattle of drums, then off they troop, supporters of no importance now the vote is in.

India's one-time dictator, Indira Gandhi, mounted a ferocious assault on India's aristocracy. Land, palace, forts were all confiscated; most are now abandoned ruins. The Jagirdar's ancient jeep is not abandoned. It is a ruin. The original engine has been replaced with a diesel engine removed from an outmoded agricultural machine. The engine thumps. It overheats. No doubt it dreams of retirement. Dusk and the majordomo drives me to view flying squirrels in the forest reserve. The majordomo shows minimum confidence in the jeep. The steering is peculiar. Hit a pothole (of which there are many) and the jeep swerves, though not in a specific direction so that foreseeing and counteracting the swerve is chance. Little wonder that the majordomo is nervous. So am I. So is the elderly retainer in the back whose job it is to top up the radiator midway.

Flying squirrels are nocturnal. If they were to fly, they would fly at night. They don't fly. They glide short distances steeply; imagine an overweight base jumper with short arms. We arrive at the flying squirrel reserve in the last minutes of the short-lived tropical dusk. We have two flashlights and a lantern. I sit on a stone bench between two large trees while the majordomo whispers to the two reserve custodians. Dusk is mosquito hour. Mosquitoes whine. Imagine a thousand Stuka fighter bombers. Flying-squirrel hour is on hand. I peer up into the tree. Flashlights shine. A small indistinguishable blob drops at an angle of 10 degrees off the vertical. A second blob drops. Much excitement…

The Jagirdar joins me for breakfast. Middle-aged, he is a tall well-set man with a serious moustache. We talk quietly of this and that, agriculture mostly, family a little. His parents and siblings prefer Delhi. Dhariyawad suits him. He is at home here, his roots well bedded and his responsibilities both pleasurable and satisfying. He, his wife and children live in apartments at the rear of the hotel. They hope to put in a swimming pool next year. The children are pre-school. Eventually they will have to go away. Hopefully his son will return.

I know various of his ilk in England, thoughtful and loyal lovers of the land. For comics, their lineage brands them as pompous dullards. Meanwhile the comics cheat on their taxes and send their children to the same schools. Well now, where did that come from?

I am riding country roads south from Dhariyawad towards Vadodara. Some villages close to Dhariyawad are Tribal – so they are called in the subcontinent where the inhabitants are judged primitive and of small social value; their lands are encroached upon and often expropriated. These Tribals are fortunate in having a patron in the Jagirdar who organises safaris to view their religious festivals. Mud walls are freshly whitewashed, thatch trimmed, Tribals neatly dressed.

Rivers and the Naglia and Jakham dams make this a rich land of watered fields. Wheat is the staple and tractors are common.

Unfortunately road signs are non-existent and asking for directions to Vadodara is met with blank stares. Vadodara is a large city with a population of two million. Distance from Dhariyawad is 300 kilometres and I am halfway. How can people not know where it is? A truck driver saves me. A few villagers gather as I interrogate him only to be met with the same blank look, then sudden comprehension, 'Ah, Baroda…'

The listeners immediately nod and murmur, 'Baroda. Baroda…'

So much for the local politicos who have sought popularity by de-Anglicising place names as in Vadodara for Baroda, Mumbai for Bombay, Chennai for Madras…

Goa beckons and I am pressed for time. Vadodara is a bed in a guest house whose owner is a retired headmaster of a local high school. We dine together, vegetarian. He complains of endemic corruption in the body politic. I leave early for the coast.

Daman is at the mouth of the Daman Ganga River 250 kilometres south of Baroda/Vadodara. The territory was ceded to the Portuguese by the Sultan of Gujarat in 1539. Prime Minister Nehru ordered the invasion of all Portuguese territories on the nineteenth of December, 1961. Thus ended 430 years of Portuguese rule. So much for history…

Modern Daman is in two halves divided by the river. Nani-Daman is a moderately chaotic mix of high-rise and bazaar, hotels, restaurants and wine shops geared to sell cheap booze to Indian males on holiday from the surrounding state of Gujarat where alcohol is forbidden.

Cross the bridge to Moti-Daman and the Portuguese fort and enter a quieter more tranquil world. Indian forts were built to guard Maharajahs and their palaces. Daman fort sheltered bureaucrats, traders and their families. No palaces here. Trees shade peaceful streets of modest buildings. Even the cathedral is little bigger than a parish church. I sit a while on a bench in the plain white nave. The Eucharist light flickers on the altar. A small elderly woman and her pre-teen granddaughter kneel and light votive candles. A plump grey-haired priest smiles welcome as he passes. I am at peace. This is my culture. I practise dying. Then back to Nani-Daman and Nana's restaurant for a splendid fish soup followed by spicy prawns.

Where am I sleeping? First I tried the Hotel Marina where polished wood floors and high ceilings of an old-style Portuguese home promised romance. An arrogant young manager showed me three rooms that smelt stale and damp. The TVs were secured in wooden cages (when did you last thieve a hotel TV?) and he demanded a 1,500-rupee deposit for a 600-rupee room. No, thanks. Better a clean room with a clean smell in a modern building at 350.

My knowledge of heroin is academic, though extensive. Thus I know that taking a hit develops a hunger for more. Prawns are similar, which explains why I am on the road early and racing south from Daman for the small seaside town of Murud. The highway is good. I cruise at 90 kph and cut inland to avoid Mumbai – why risk bronchitis?

I pull in beside a sextet of cops for directions on which road to take.

An officer asks my age.

'Seventy-seven, seventy-eight next week.' I show him my passport.

The cops hand my passport round, yak and laugh amongst themselves. Are they going to hit me with a fine for something? No, they are giving me an advance birthday present: permission to ride up the Pune (or Poona) Expressway (illegal for bikes). The police tell me which exit to take, that the exit road leads to a T-junction where a restaurant on the corner serves good food.

A little weird being the only biker on a six-lane highway, somehow vulnerable, defenceless – if that makes sense. Ignoring the restaurant strikes me as bad manners: fresh lime and soda and a bowl of Mongolian soup…

The right-hand arm of the T-junction leads to Pale and so to the coast. Murud is more of a large village than a town. Fishing and tourism are the main pursuits. The offshore fortress of Janjira is the main attraction – apart from fresh seafood. I am staying at the Seashore Resort, listed in guidebooks as having three rooms, a pretty garden, and run by a friendly family – accurate, though one room is closed while they extend the main house. I didn't find the place through the guidebook. The doorman at a posh hotel across the street recommended it. A German family occupy the second room. Mother is a retired teacher. Father, a mathematician, is about to be retired with a golden handshake by a software company; younger people are available at half his salary. In her mid-twenties, the daughter is cogitating on a career in what might loosely be described as the social services (or good deeds). They are travelling by hire car with a driver. They laugh a lot, love each other and read books. Good neighbours…

My room has three beds. Pile all three mattresses on one bed and you have three layers of rock. Walk down the garden and you are on the beach.

Two of my guidebooks recommend the same restaurant, Patil Khanaval. The restaurant is listed as on the seafront. Murud must have expanded since the researchers visited. Now the restaurant is down an alley. The cook is dug out of bed. He runs through the menu whilst picking his nose: fish biriyani, mutton biriyani, prawn biriyani. He may be a great chef but the nose is a negative. Better a Muslim restaurant with tables in a large garden the shore side of the shore road. Fish soup and grilled prawns, delicious. And so to my bed of layered rocks…

Dawn in the garden at the Seashore Resort, Murud. A cool breeze off the sea stirs palm fronds overhead. Crows pick through the night's rubbish discarded on the beach. Bath water heats on an open fire. The resort's elderly henna-haired jack-of-all-trades brings coffee and chai. The tide is out and the German family and I watch bullock carts race each other along the glistening sand. Drivers whip the beasts and yell – all but a young lad bringing up the rear. Of his two bullocks, one is big and grey and staid. The second is small and young and tries to trot whilst the elder plods. The driver leans right forward and whacks the young bullock. For trotting or for not trotting fast enough? The driver ignores the old bullock. The older bullock ignores the driver.

The German family depart. They are good people, well read and thoughtful, against the Iraq War, doubtful of involvement in Afghanistan, critical of Britain's subservience to the United States. The mother photographed the bullock race. The father downloaded the pictures to my computer. Why did he download a picture of his daughter? Surely not a subconscious hope that she might find a husband through my blog...

Murud is a pleasant town for a stroll, small, compact, tranquil. Inhabitants are polite; streets are dirt and narrow, buildings mostly low and old. Mango trees and coconut palms offer shade. The small covered market overflows with fruit and vegetables. Muslim women cloaked in black speak softly to each other as they pick and choose. I am no foot fetishist, yet sandalled feet awaken fantasies; young feet, a toe ring, henna pattern across the instep, powdery dirt yielding beneath thin leather soles. So different from the barefoot Hindu woman bearing baskets of sand on their heads to a building site on the beach side of the road. Breeze off the sea tugs at thin cotton saris; temptation a glimpse of pale mahogany bellies varnished with sweat. Safer is watching fisherman mending nets...

Seated at a waterfront café, I sip fresh lime and soda (no sugar, no salt). For the past hour some 40 men have been talking together on stone benches in the beachfront park next door. Most are elderly. I watch now as they walk down the beach. They hitch their pants a few inches and paddle a few feet out from the shore. Four young Bombayites at the next table tell me that the men are scattering a friend's ashes. For a friend they should have paddled further and made sure the tide was on the ebb. Or perhaps they planned having their friend's ashes stick to their ankles...

Heading south tomorrow, I must take a ferry from Janjira across an inlet. Janjira is separated from Murud by a creek and a steep treeless hill that rises directly from the shore. Janjira nestles in a cleft in the hill. Cross the bridge and ride up the hill and you look down on a nest of coconut palms sheltering pan-tiled cottages and a mosque. Fishing boats lie offshore and the great walls of Janjira Fort rise dark from the waters. Some say that pirates from the Horn of Africa built the fort in the eleventh century and it was never subdued. Were the builders Somali? Certainly Muslim, and Janjira remains a Muslim village. Veiled women in black peek at me from doorways...

Riding a bike is a solitary occupation. I have time to think. Subjects of thought return again and again, become familiar companions and refuse to be abandoned until written down. So here is a thought on police, of whom I ask directions in whatever country I travel. I come of a generation (and perhaps a class) that considers the police as one of the four solid foundation blocks of the community. The vicar or priest cared for our souls; the doctor cared for our health; the family lawyer shared with the bank manager a care for our finances; the policeman was our protector and the protector of our property; laws were passed for our benefit. Why then do my children's generations view the police as the enemy? And if the police are the enemy of youth, what youth joins the police? This last is a serious and disturbing question. And that is enough on the subject – though I will return to it. But now is the hour to daub my face and ankles with mosquito repellent and stroll down Murud's shore street, bid its citizens (other than the veiled) *good evening*, sip a fresh lime and soda and decide in which restaurant to dine. Prawns? Probably...

I have a great affection for ferries. The smaller the ferry, the more romantic. The Janjira ferry is a decked launch. Passengers sit on benches or on the roof. Eight motorbikes is the maximum wheeled cargo. Steep steps lead down to the quay, a narrow pathway bisects the steps. The angle of descent exceeds 45 degrees. The specialist from the ferry takes the bike keys and rides the bike down.

Four men lift the bike into the launch. The engineer starts the diesel engine and we thrum out to sea past fishing boats tugging at anchors. Heat haze softens the great grey fortification and makes of Janjira Fort a mirage floating on the water. Definitely romantic. As always on a boat or ship, we passengers, thrown together, fall into conversation. From where do I come? To where am I travelling? What of my family? So ask dark, smiling, friendly men, while I ask how the road is. Mundane? Yes. But warming for a lone traveller, a charging of batteries that will last a day in the saddle.

The country road from the Janjira ferry south twists through steep wooded hills and through river valleys – a glorious ride. I don't think of myself as a biker. I don't have the leathers or the decals. I've only changed a tyre once and I prefer paying a mechanic to adjust the chain. It's not laziness or incompetence, more that I enjoy watching a professional at his work and enjoy the usual crowd that frequents a bike mechanic's shop. Imagine those hours in Jaisalmer watching the Sikh brothers rebuild the antique Enfield's motor.

This is beginning to read as an apology for enjoying myself. Not so. It is simply that I am surprised at the fun I get from biking (given that I don't think of myself as a biker), and given that most people on the road (foreign or Indian) think that my riding a bike round India is remarkable. Most are surprised that I've survived. True, I was in shock the first couple of weeks. India's traffic obeys neither laws nor logic, however it does have a rhythm – or that's what I feel. Get with the rhythm and you enjoy the ride. Or perhaps the third fresh lime and soda has gone to my head. Maybe I should stick with beer…

I am an idiot. I have broken one of the cardinal rules: *Never never ever ever ride at night.* No excuses. And it might have killed me. It nearly did. The country road from the Janjira ferry connects with the N17 highway to Goa. The N17 is a great road for a biker: hill sections with luscious curves to lean into, straight stretches shaded by overhanging trees, bridges over dreamland rivers, a good surface, great places to stop for coffee and a bowl of soup.

Ratnagiri is the only large town. Large is all that can be said for Ratnagiri. The town is 15 kilometres off the highway. Late afternoon and I ride midway through the outskirts for an ATM and a top-up for my mobile. Hotels are modern and probably expensive. I noticed a hotel at the highway intersection so I turn back. The hotel is a real dump: check out a room and hear an anticipatory rustle from the bed bugs. I know that I should ride back into town but what the hell, there's bound to be something better and I ride on into the twilight. The next place, 10 kilometres further, is worse and night has fallen. I've been riding all day; my visor is smudged with grease and dirt and I'm blinded by oncoming traffic. Hill country and two buses race at me neck and neck uphill on a tight curve. No white line as a guide and I can't see a damn thing. The front wheel kicks over a stone as I go off the road. Brake and I'm done for. The buses thunder by and I fight the bike back on to the black top. Luck saves me from hitting a tree or a rock. I'm scared shitless (as they say in impolite circles) and I'm cursing myself. I bring the bike to a halt and wait while my breathing steadies. No mosquitoes and I would try sleeping beneath a tree. And snakes…

Twenty kilometres brings me to a small town with two small hotels. The hotels are either full or Reception hates my looks. My hands tremble as I drink a coffee and wash the visor and my spectacles. Better…

A further 15 kilometres and an ultra-modern hotel appears on the left – so new that the builders haven't finished surfacing the approach road. This is a flash joint that has to be 2,000 rupees a night. I'd pay 10,000 to get off the road. The owner wears six chunky gold rings and a welcoming smile. The room has air conditioning, hot water, brilliant mattress and flat-screen satellite TV with CNN and BBC World Service. Dinner is chicken masala with both basmati rice and chapatis. Breakfast is included in the 600-rupee room rate! I lie in bed and call Bernadette. I don't mention riding by night or coming off the road. One near-death experience is sufficient…

Back home I cross the hills to Malvern most days and swim at the

Malvern Spa. Today I head for Malvan where I intend spending the night. Malvan is on the coast. It is reputed to have a fine beach. It is a few kilometres north of the Goa state boundary. Tomorrow I will ride up into the mountains to sleep in the cool of a little-visited hill resort, Amboli, from where a side road circles down to Goa's capital.

Goa is full of ancient memories. I delay my arrival for fear of what I will discover, not so much in Goa as in myself. I was callous then. Callous and a coward. I had broken out of jail, on the run from a life sentence. My jailers were a wife I loved and two small children whom I adored. Did I think of them? Yes, often, and with tears.

National Highway 17 is a biker's dream. I am repeating myself for the benefit of readers who suffer from memory deficiency or laid this book aside for a week or two. It is a climb-and-dip road with curves to lean into. Forest cloaks the hills. Neem trees shade the straight stretches. Coconut palms shade riverbanks. I stop a while to watch a limited overs cricket match. Our village club back home has two county-quality grass fields, all-weather practice nets, bowling machine, pavilion with a bar. Twenty spectators on a Saturday afternoon and we are doing well. Here the field is dry rice paddy. No pads or gloves for batsmen, no helmets, and I am one of 50 spectators seated on the roadside. A further 50 or more spectators are dotted round the boundaries. Fast bowlers at either end; batsmen drive the ball along the ground; a close-in paddy bank does the fielding. Batsman go for the aerial route. My fellow spectators try communicating with me. The few words we share are cricket terminology: leg before, boundary, catch. Too glorious a morning to be depressed by the language barrier. We make do with smiles...

Turn west off the NH17 at Kasal and Malvan is 26 kilometres down a twisty lane across paddy and past houses sheltered by mango, jack fruit and coconut. Bananas, guavas and papaya grow in the yards. Spit out a seed and it sprouts. Malvan is one narrow crowded higgledy-piggledy street blocked by a couple of buses and a builder's truck. Carry on a few kilometres and you reach the Tarkarli

Peninsula promoted by the Maharashtra Tourism Board as India's Tahiti. Gauguin would have been disappointed – no bare breasts. Houses are larger closer to the beach and more numerous – holiday homes. A few advertise family home-stay for respectable Indian families. The Maharashtra Tourist Development Corporation owns and runs the only hotel. It is easy to find. Governments excel at signboards. They are less good at service industries and the MTDC resort on the Tarkarli Peninsula suffers from the dread hand of state ownership. A brick path leads up through casuarina pines to a scattering of simple cottages and an open-sided restaurant. Some of the bricks on the path are missing and rubbish needs removing. A large air-conditioning unit protrudes from the rear of each cottage. Glance up and the cottages appear hunchbacked.

I sit at a table outside the restaurant. Three members of staff ignore me. No matter, the deserted beach is white sand licked by blue sea and stretches way into the distance – bliss for beach lovers. I drag off my boots, stick my socks in my pocket, roll up my pants and paddle. The sea is cool. The sand is too hot for bare feet and roasts my backside when I sit to pull my boots back on. The restaurant staff are in the same conversation. I wait patiently and wonder whether I really want to stay the night. Would a climb up the coastal escarpment to Amboli be more satisfying?

Victory! Or victory of a sort… A waiter has taken my order for lime and soda and a fried pomfret (flat fish somewhat akin to a sole).

The waiter assures me that the fish is fresh. True – and delicious. Sadly the rice is precooked and rancid and the bill for the fish is 50 per cent higher than the price on the menu.

The waiter claims that it was a big fish. Yes, in competition with sprats.

Memories surface of state-run restaurants in Cuba. Four years of Cuba was sufficient. Amboli, here I come…

Amboli is 690 metres above sea level. The road zigzags up a thickly forested mountainside. It is a good road with stone parapets. Monkeys sit on the parapet where passing children throw them half-eaten bananas. Drivers park below a waterfall and wash their trucks. Indian tourists photograph the view with mobile phones. The view would be clear in Hispanic America. In India a haze is standard – or standard in the bits of India through which I've travelled on this journey. This isn't a complaint, more a point of interest. I will head north to the Himalayas later. Will the views be clear?

Amboli isn't a town. It isn't even a village – certainly not an Indian village. Indian villages have a main street lined with kiosks. Amboli is a scattering of unplanned low-rise concrete construction, a few holiday homes but mostly featureless hotels in the 20-room bracket – not many of them but sufficient to make Amboli a visual disaster. *Lonely Planet* advises that tourists can visit bauxite mines. Maybe I'm picky but bauxite mines don't register as major attractions. Come on, old man, be courageous, take the memory lane to Goa. Confront your past.

My Eicher road atlas is much admired by fellow travellers. Page 98 shows a small road south from Amboli to Ramghat, Bhedshi and Maneri where it joins the highway to Panjim, Goa's capital. The road starts well, single track but good tar, and runs across a rocky plateau through dense forest. The trees are small but the canopy is solid and a deep green. The air is fresh and scented. After the disappointment of Amboli, heaven. I check with a passing bicyclist: 'Ramghat?'

Negative. But what does he know.

Next, an elderly gentleman on a motorcycle: 'Ramghat? Panjim? Goa?'

Negative.

Perhaps he is stupid.

Two pedestrian countrymen wave me down. No need for words. Their gestures suffice. The road ends. Oh…

So ends prevarication. Backtrack down the escarpment to the NH17 and ride on across the state border into Goa.

7

BIRTHDAY GOA

My memories are of Calangute as a small village, 50 foreigners at most. Fishermen mending nets were the only Indians. Now Calangute is the northern end of a 30-kilometre hodgepodge of high-rise apartment blocks, bed-bug doss houses, luxury resorts, bars and restaurants ranging in quality from brilliant to instant dysentery.

I trust to luck in searching for my past. The luck is an Italian with a shack restaurant amongst the trees a kilometre back from Vagator Beach. He has long hair, an ancient Enfield and spent years up in Poona or Pune at the Shri Rajneesh ashram. Wow! A real-life *sannyasin,* mid-sixties and an old stager. He belongs – while I fall at the first hurdle. Imagine! I've never heard of Prem Joshua, never listened to his music, the true sound of Goa (so the Italian assures me). Prem Joshua is in concert tonight on the beach north towards Arambol. Everybody will be there. I should return to the restaurant after the concert for prawn risotto. The risotto is an invitation.

Everybody at the Prem Joshua concert is a small crowd of maybe 100, of whom the vast majority are foreign; the few Indians are from Bombay. The true sound of Goa is German with a pigtail. He sits in splendour on a raised dais on the stage and plays the sitar and a flute. To his right, a grey-haired Japanese with a frozen face plays bass electric guitar next to a tabla player who might be Indian. A second German plays keyboard and fiddles with a laptop. Prem Joshua is both serious and spiritual. He dedicates his songs to a series of Sufi saints and mystics. My untrained ear finds one song much like the next – were Sufi mystics equally similar? Not that I recall. The concert is enlivened on occasion by all four musicians emitting a series of very loud harsh barks.

The Japanese bass player runs out of battery.

I clap once at the wrong moment.

The prawn risotto is not an invitation. It is dry, without taste and ridiculously overpriced. Luck is a young Dutch couple at the next table, Fiona and Paul. They have been residents in Goa for the past two years, renting a house a few kilometres inland from the coast.

I was a guest my last night in England at the Taj Group's hotel on Buckingham Palace Road – the outrageously opulent prime minister's suite with God knows how many rooms including a library, study, drawing room and the most suave and kindly of Romanian butlers. Christmas was the suite in the delightful Usha Kiran Palace. Jodhpur was the wondrous art deco Umaid Bhawan. Today is my birthday and I am at the Taj Hotel Group's beach resort in Goa.

Yesterday one of the resort managers drove me up to the Portuguese fort on the point. Rather than a courtesy car, we used the resort's work jeep. They don't think of me as a guest, the manager explained, but as a member of the Taj family. It is for this as much as for the pampering that I wish to offer gratitude – not only for being made to feel part of a family but of a family of which I am proud.

I am writing this in the private garden of my guest cottage at the resort. A waiter has delivered a chocolate birthday cake with candles and a card. The young manager of yesterday drops by. A Catholic Goan, he has degrees in everything from law to ecology. I remark that my only disappointment on this journey is my inability to communicate, to question.

'You can ask me anything…'

'No, I can't.'

'Yes, you can.'

'I can't. I don't want to embarrass you.'

'You won't embarrass me.'

'Yes, I will.'

'You won't.'

So, and reluctantly, 'How much did Goa's chief of police pay for his job?'

Silence...

'I told you that I'd embarrass you.' Anyway I knew the answer – and the resulting tragedy: that the chief of police is appointed for six years... Six years in which to recuperate his very substantial capital outlay and make a profit. Thus from the newest constable right up through superintendents, all are corrupted by the necessity of paying off the chief of police.

Is writing the above a farewell to further visas?

Perhaps such fear explains my delay in bringing this journal to its conclusion. I love India. I have so many friends in the subcontinent. Forbidden to return would be a great sadness.

My birthday continues with an invitation from the Dutch couple, Fiona and Paul, to dine at a Burmese restaurant, Bomras, for dinner. The dinner is as fine as any I have eaten. Prawns? Naturally – raw tuna, tender beef, a Burmese chicken salad, et cetera, et cetera. Plus a gently lethal but delicious drink, the Bomras special.

From Bomras, we continue to the holiday home of a wealthy young Delhiite. Architecture is ultra-modern; the living room with a wall of glass borders a lagoon, water reflecting overhanging trees. An Italian male struts his stuff in golden shoes and platinum self-regard. Two young women, Brits from west London via Solihull, grandparents from the subcontinent, coo their admiration of Italian men. Italian men have such wonderful taste.

The Italian preens while the wicked ones extend their admiration to cover every aspect of male peacock self-adulation. Perhaps an hour passes before doubt creeps beneath the Italian's carapace. Doubt turns to certainty. He flees. His persecutors prance in victory. The Dutch drop me back at the Taj. Wash, teeth in a glass, heart medication, read birthday emails from my children then lie in bed and call Bernadette. I wish she were here.

But a good birthday, one of the best.

Fiona and Paul – is it sexist to put the woman's name ahead of the man's? Or the man's ahead of the woman's? Please excuse the digression. I have had only one cup of coffee this morning and my thoughts remain somewhat disorganised.

So, to continue, Fiona and Paul have invited me to stay. This Dutch couple may not be the true voice of Goa. They are the true voice of modern India. They research the Asian automotive market and provide detailed reports for major motor manufacturers. They founded their company 15 years ago with offices in Delhi, moved to Bangalore and now to Goa. A large Portuguese country house is both their home and their office where employees sit at computer terminals in what was the dining room. The guest bedroom is as big as a UK council flat. The bathroom is marginally smaller. I sleep in an emperor-sized bed beneath a mosquito net. I keep the door to the corridor shut. Leave it open and the room is invaded by a pack of ex-stray dogs and puppies.

Paul and Fiona work from home. They don't eat in. They haven't eaten in for 15 years. They could write the definitive guide to the best restaurants in Delhi, Bangalore and Goa without further research – a fresh project should they lose interest in automobiles. They are also the experts on India's stray dog population. Fiona and Paul groom strays. Spot a male stray and the grooming begins with leftovers from dinner. A week and the stray becomes expectant. Progress to physical contact. Finally into the back of the car and home to the knife and recuperation. Two such dedicated castrators per district would decimate India's huge stray-dog population. Mrs Gandhi tried doing it with *Homo sapiens*.

Paul and Fiona work a 12-hour day. I hunt my past. Goa's hippy community has been squeezed steadily northward. Calangute was the beginning, then Baga, Anjuna... Now 90 minutes up the coast to Arambol. Goa is ruined – so they say. Then why do I pass almost deserted white-sand beaches?

As to the hunt, imagine a fat elderly blimp accosting any oldie with long hair. 'Excuse me, have you been here long?'

In a guttural German accent, 'Ten years…'

The Brit Blimp needs 40 … And the courage to keep accosting elderly long-haired strangers. A full day (unsuccessful) and I divide those I ask into gracious, puzzled, bewildered, dismissive and impolite.

Initiated by Susan and Grant Johnson, a Canadian couple, www.horizonsunlimited.com is an internet community of biker travellers. Check the hubb for road conditions in Albania, visas for Turkmenistan, possibility of entering China, BMW mechanic in Buenos Aires, whatever – you'll find it here. And you make friends. I have been communicating via the web with an English couple, Lisa and Simon, since 2004. Now, finally, we meet on Arambol Beach. They have been on the road for seven years and ride BMW monsters. Travel ecstasy for me is good tar, a dish of prawns, soft mattress, clean bathroom and emails from my kids. Simon and Lisa are adventurous. The tougher the road, the happier. Truly dangerous and they are ecstatic. Check their site on how to survive a broken neck in the Amazon forest (www.2ridetheworld.com). However a few weeks of Indian drivers has put Simon in a hate-India mood.

He takes his hatred out on the sand, gouging tight turns and hard-throttle tyre-spinning. Lunch under a straw canopy is calmer. Simon and Lisa have difficulties in getting published. Simon does the writing and organises their photo library while Lisa does the more mundane: route planning, visas, finance, etc. Simon is one more 40-year-old biker – OK, so he's tall with long hair and moderately glamorous. Who cares? Lisa is the story. She is the elder by 10 years, tough good-looking without being butch and astride a great big throbbing BMW. Open the throttle and she leaves Simon trailing. That's the story, *Flash Leather and a Toy Boy*. Many a woman's dream.

I don't do parties in the UK. Eight people in a room is a maximum. More and I become claustrophobic. Cocktail parties are my particular hate. Stand with a drink in one hand, nibbles in the other and nod intelligently to someone whom you can't hear above the general babble. And what do you do with the trash? Leave with a pocket full of toothpicks and olive stones? Outdoors is different, room to breathe and usually somewhere to sit. This party is hosted by a Bombayite and his English lady companion, friends of Fiona and Paul. I sit on a stone parapet of comfortable height and talk with a Goan civil engineer. Does he know of a Goan architect with a Danish wife?

De Souza – yes, of course. He is dead: she is back in Denmark with their daughter. The son, Amin, lives here in Panjim.

I recall Amin as a small boy.

'We'll telephone him,' encourages the engineer.

'At 10 o'clock?'

Absolutely – and he does. 'Amin, I have someone here who wants to talk to you,' and hands me his mobile.

'Amin, you won't remember me. Simon Gandolfi.'

'Simon Gandolfi! Of course I remember. You used to drive us to the beach in your open Volkswagen…'

Why did Amin de Souza remember me? With this thought, my own memory clicks into gear. I know my present host – or used to know him. I recall visiting his home in Bombay more than once. He was married in those days to a difficult German.

The garden lights are dim – though good light would be of little help; 40 years changes a man. 'Simon Gandolfi,' I say, introducing myself. 'You manufactured the belts for Peter Henry and the silver snake belt scam.'

Peter Henry was a Brit and an accomplished and imaginative scam artist. Antique Indian silver snake belts were a fashion item in Europe and North America and young Westerners on their travels were scouring the bazaars for belts. Peter Henry spotted a short cut. Surely snake belts were as easy to manufacture as metal watch straps. In those days my present host owned a steel watch-strap factory in

Bombay. Peter Henry ordered a few hundred silver snake belts. He packed the belts in a net and buried them in the sand a short way above the low water mark. Two weeks and the belts had gained the wear of a century. Peter Henry headed for New York in time for Christmas, reaped a splendid profit and swamped the market. Snake belts were finished as a fashion item.

Now, 40 years later: 'What happened to Peter Henry?' asks my host.

Last I knew of him, Peter was in Liverpool preparing designs for a flash Chinese restaurant and overseeing the work. The Chinese paid Peter up front – always an error with Peter. So is scamming the Chinese. Peter disappeared. That was 30 years ago and Liverpool is a sea port. The tide goes out twice a day. Those of us who knew Peter well fear that he went out on the tide. However, Peter was a great survivor. Perhaps he is doing a Gauguin in Tahiti.

My turn now to question my host: What happened to Walking John?

Walking John was a Brit in his late twenties. His base was a bed-sit with bathroom on Bombay's Marine Drive – nowadays as costly as a walk on the moon. John wintered in Goa and summered trekking in the Himalayas. John liked to tell of his walking and Peter Henry was a listener. One of John's tales concerned the Buddhist monastery closest to Base Camp on Mount Everest. The monks had become rich and lazy on the leavings of Everest expeditions. In earlier days they survived on the sale of religious prints on handmade paper. Climate made printing difficult. Either the inks froze or humidity made the inks bleed. According to Walking John printing was possible only six weeks a year.

Eastern Spirituality was big business in the sixties. Peter Henry loaded John and two young Californian women with natural colour inks and handmade paper bought at an art supply store in Bombay and instructed John to reach the monastery at the beginning of the climate window, rent the blocks from the monks and print, print, print.

Peter Henry took the prints to New York for Christmas and set up a display (at Bergdorf Goodman, if I remember correctly) with photographs of Everest and the monastery, monks coached to look spiritual and a few monastic gewgaws – one was a silver-edged bowl fashioned from a human cranium.

Genuine Buddhist prints from the Monastery at Everest Base Camp and blessed by the abbot made a great Christmas present at $100. The outlay was five cents. Walking John complained that he never saw the profit. Such is the risk in joining forces with a scam artist.

So where is Walking John now?

'Almost certainly in Goa,' says my host. He adds that John is married to a Goan woman, daughter of a fisherman – implying that neither she nor John are socially acceptable. Getting John's telephone number may take a few days.

Amin de Souza has invited me to lunch. We will meet at the steps below Panjim's biggest church. I arrive early, park the bike and sit in the cool of the nave. I am digging into happenings that have lain heavily on me for 40 years – surely an inappropriate time to practise dying.

I imagine death as a rosebud opening to release the spirit. Cling to life and the rosebud shrivels and becomes a prison. Hence the need to practise letting go. Churches have the right atmosphere in which to practise.

So here I go, seated on a wooden bench, eyes closed, hands lightly clasped and concentrating on being thankful for a full life. Not giving thanks to anyone or to any God – simply being thankful, appreciative. And reminding myself that the body is a jail, that death is release and should be welcomed joyously as the route to being reabsorbed into the Oneness from which we come. I am keen on the Oneness and balk at the God word. And I am not suggesting here that we should be in a hurry to die…

So, protected by the massive walls of the church, I surrender to the quiet and cool and peace, surely a delightful hors d'oeuvres for luncheon with Amin…

I sit and say little but, at peace, listen to the history of his life, of a father increasingly erratic and increasingly frail to whom, in nursing, Amin gave chunks of his life and on whose death, Amin managed to clean, if not the emotional distress his father bequeathed, at least the financial chaos.

It seems to me, as I listen, that suffering from his father's actions and the collapse of his parent's marriage, then suffering for his father in his illness has made Amin very self-contained. He has tested himself and learned the futility of anger. He has become a man to trust, a man of remarkable integrity, a man good to be with.

Fiona and Paul are giving a Sunday luncheon at a French restaurant on the beach. Of their guests, I am the only non-Indian. A major industrialist with homes here in Goa and in Delhi and Bombay and in France and New York (two) talks of the British in the years after Indian Independence. He lists companies then famous in British industry, all surrendered to Indian ownership. Britain had lost interest in India. British industry sent their weakest managers.

I doubt whether British managers existed who could have saved British industries in India. If so, why didn't they save British industry at home? Car manufacturers deceased. Truck manufacturers deceased. Locomotive manufacturers deceased. Motorcycle manufacturers deceased. And so on and so on and so on…

Midday and the cloister of a village church offers sanctuary from the heat. Lunch is fresh lime soda and fresh fish on the terrace at a corner café from where I watch men digging a trench along the road edge. Impossible to tell how old are the skin-and-bones women in thin saris who bear away the spoil – 25 or 55? How many hours do they work? How many children have they borne?

Men hike the baskets on to the women's heads. Basket leakage mixes with the women's sweat, naked shoulders sun-sheened. Off they sway. Next, next, next… While tourists buzz by on motor scooters, cool in the breeze and unseeing of the female ant-trail barefoot on the hot tar. Why am I so angry on such a perfect day?

And I've left my guidebook in the church cloister. Old fool…

The guidebook is gone. I knock on the presbytery door. The priest and four students are at lunch at a square table set with a white tablecloth edged with lace. A student is dispatched to fetch my guidebook from the priest's office. The priest is elderly, probably native Portuguese. A kind face, gentle. How not to imagine his pain, he as sullied by his fellow priests' vice as we Brits, all of us, are sullied by the wickedness of Abu Ghraib from which grew hatred of the West. An old-fashioned ceiling fan paddles the air…

The erstwhile manufacturer of silver snake belts telephones with a number for Walking John. I call and we meet at John's house. It seems to me a sad house, old and long and narrow and dark and neglected. John bought the house many years ago as a restoration project. Restoration stalled early.

And John, though 10 years the younger, seems to me old.

We sit opposite sides of a wood table in the dimly lit entrada and he tells me of his health. He has cataracts, and had a cancer cut out from close to his nose but too close to his eyes for radiotherapy. Whether the surgeon removed all the cancer is uncertain. John has wondered often what happened to me, so he says, and talks of me often to those he sees from the old days. He commiserates with me for having arrived too late for last month's reunion of Goa's old stagers – though most who came were from the seventies or later. John shows me a book commemorating the reunion with photographs of then and now. Long hair is the uniting feature. The faces are foreign to me. Even when here, I wasn't part of that. The inside cover lists the dead. Few of the names are familiar. Alejandro, yes. None of the others.

John seems stuck in the past while I have moved on. Yet, there, at his table, a single question from Walking John hurtles me back

40 years. Did I know that Vanessa had died shortly after she and I parted?

Vanessa, who I have been trying to trace on the worldwide web…

I bid my farewells to Walking John and ride back to Calangute. The beach is thickly speckled with Indian day-trippers. A thinner rash of paddlers speckles the sea close in. The house we rented all those years ago is a beach bar. The storeroom was our bedroom – Vanessa's and mine. It was sufficiently wide to take our mattress lengthwise with space at the foot of the bed for our possessions. We had a workman lay the cement floor. Clothes hung on a wire strung across one corner. Now crates of empty beer bottles lean stacked against the rear wall.

I stand there amongst the garbage, a fresh lime soda in hand. The memories flood in. Of Vanessa, sarong knotted above her breasts, walking up the beach the day we met. We travelled together, our journey Vanessa's as much as mine. We were good together. Certainly there was love – yet I abandoned her in Nepal. I was taking that wrong road and didn't want her involved. What remains of that period is a hoard of secret memories, remorse, a few stories.

I visualise the young French girl seated at the end of our mattress, bobbed blond, too thin yet classically beautiful. A heroin addict, she seemed so vulnerable as she asked our permission to shoot up; she feared to be alone as she hit. I picture her now as she licked the needle as if it were her lover – I with a terror of needles; five years old when a course of injections killed my father; I overheard our nanny speak of it.

I remember four of us driving through Mapusa in the open VW, turning right at the end of the market to head back to Calangute and hearing someone call my name. None of the others heard the shout. I reversed back round the corner. An old friend, Hamish Crawford, sick with jaundice, swayed on the sidewalk. He hadn't called my name. He had seen the VW pull away round the corner and thought that, were I in India, it was the sort of car I would drive. Mapusa market is unrecognisable.

There was Slugs Jerry's tame guru who cured two Canadian girls of gonorrhoea with prayer, meditation, herbal potions and the antibiotics secreted at the bottom of his Ayurvedic medicine chest.

And trying to meet Blind George one perfect morning, he walking through the palm trees back from Baga Beach and I walking in the opposite direction. George, with only 10 per cent peripheral vision, faced 45 degrees from the direction of his walk and someone had fed me a powerful cookie for breakfast. Calculating a point of intersection was beyond us.

And of course the arrest of Caroline for nakedness on the beach and the gold smuggler paying her fine. And always Vanessa. And always remorse. Enough...

Except to thank Fiona and Paul for their company and for their kindness and generosity. Stray dogs are their normal house guests. A fat old snoring Brit on a bike was an extra.

8

SOUTH FROM GOA

From Panaji, Goa's capital, to Cochin in Kerala is one thousand kilo-metres. I am on the road three days. Three days of memories, of the open VW, Vanessa bronzed, hair fluffed by the breeze. This is the road we took. The brick factory on the left is familiar, boys empty-ing baskets of clay into a press, the pressed clay extruded and cut by a guillotine; hesitate and the man retrieving each brick loses a hand. A cough would do it, a sneeze – perhaps a fly alighting on his nose.

Casuarina pines divide the road from the beach. Back then, we parked the open car on the roadside without fear of thieves. A mile or more of pale unmarked golden beach stretched left and right, sea calm and blue over a sand bottom; no one to offend or excite with our nakedness as we swam and dried ourselves in the sun before returning to the road. The road is wider now. Massive road signs point to beachfront hotels, new jobs, a better life for many, yet the brick factory is unaltered.

I stop for the night at a modern commercial hotel on a highway intersection. One table in the vast dining room is occupied by Indian businessmen. An elderly Caucasian sits at another. May I join him?

Certainly.

A Professor of Sanskrit from Pennsylvania, he is midway through a lecture tour of India's universities. He is an admirer of President Obama. He warns, however, that the president has two demerits for the mass of Americans. Firstly Obama speaks good English, proof of elitism. Americans preferred the familiar error-strewn talk of Bush, the common man.

And Obama pauses to consider before responding to a question – judged by the average citizen as a sure mark of weakness.

To my left tower the forested flanks of the Western Ghats. I am riding the coastal road. Kerala is humid here on the littoral. Skins are darker. Villages merge one into another along the highway. Houses are small and shaded by mango trees and coconut palms, tiled roofs or palm thatch, scent of dried fish and cumin, buses on the charge, the aggressive blare of klaxons. No sidewalks and villagers seem small and vulnerable. The women's saris supply splashes of colour; plastic hairbands school hip-length hair smoothed and shinning with coconut butter. And such eyes, so bright in the young, teeth a brilliant white, sadly faded in the old, beetle-rotted gums grown toothless while men, with their ever-present bidis, trail thin skeins of tobacco smoke…

Cochin had become Kochi. I don't understand Kochi. I can't place anything. My memories are of a small ferry to an island in the harbour and a sweeper forever brushing dead leaves from the hand-clipped lawns surrounding the government rest house. This was a grand wooden building guarded by great trees. Windows were tall with louvred shutters through which sunlight seeped to disturb a sombre interior of high ceilings, floors buffed to a dark sheen. Prior to British India, this was home to the Portuguese governor or the Dutch governor – I don't recall which, perhaps both. Vanessa and I stayed a week. A gently turning fan cooled our large room. Mosquito netting draped the four-poster bed. Breakfast was on a tray, dinner in a darkly solemn dining room so quiet that we talked in whispers as lovers should. Tablecloths and table napkins were white and crisply ironed. An elderly servant served fish and vegetable curries, fresh mangoes and coconut water. The few other guests were government officials. A narrow steam launch took us on day trips, slipping through shady canals carpeted in lilies and water hyacinth where small boys in mini canoes herded flocks of duck. Lord, but it was beautiful – and we the only foreigners.

Now the once-small shore-side city, Ernakulam, has sprouted shopping malls and high rises while the old town (the fort) at the mouth of the immense harbour has become a tourist magnet. Narrow tree-shaded streets that once were romantic in their mysteries are lined with hostels, hotels, curio shops, travel and tour agents. Panama-hatted foreigners pale in neat chinos and summer shirts shelter from the heat on shaded terraces. Tanned youth are more adventurous in their dress; popular are thin baggy pants of tribal origin and loose sleeveless tops, women's breasts part visible; henna-patterned feet in skinny-strapped sandals, underarm hair, tattoos, spots, mosquito bites.

The government rest house where we stayed is barely recognisable in its present guise as a five star hotel and has lost its charm. I have found a clean bed and shower in a modern guest house; bad architecture makes air conditioning necessary; romantic old-build, though more central, would be more expensive and accompanied by cockroaches in the bathroom.

Riding a bike in India is tiring. This is not a complaint. I am having a great time. However even a good night's sleep between clean sheets followed by a cold shower and breakfast dosa are insufficiently energising to hunt an internet café with effective connection. India's image as the burning tip of high-tech web development is fraudulent. A terrapin on crutches would be quicker. Uploading pictures is a lottery. Bet on which comes first, a power cut or provider overload...

I have three days in Kochi waiting for Betty de Swann to sashay off the plane. Betty is a Dutch doctor. She is gay and married to a New Zealand former super-athlete who has borne them two brilliant children by AI. My relationship with Betty was born of a shared flight from the Dominican Republic to Cuba that landed at the wrong airport. In her medical practice, Betty is good with knives; she imagines herself a rally driver when at the wheel and believes that Third World rental staff never examine the underside of a car for fear of dirtying their suits. We have bounced boulder to boulder up Caribbean riverbeds and over rocks in the Philippines. Fortunately Rio Janeiro was cabs. Now we will travel by train and chauffeur in search of tigers in the hills. Meanwhile I cross the harbour by ferry to non-tourist Ernakulam in search of a non-tourist priced meal from a menu designed to please locals. The restaurant is large, every table filled with businessmen with expanding bellies. Food is delicious. So is a store that sells an extraordinary variety of wonderful cottons. A one-room tailor in Jew Town makes three lengths up into pants at £2.50 a pair.

Betty is in India for the first time. India is tigers. The hunt is organised by a charming travel agent on Kochi's waterfront, our destination a wildlife sanctuary high on the long spine of forested hills that bisects southern India. We take a train north. A chauffeur with a cream Ambassador meets us at the station. The highway up into the hills is excellent with S bend following S bend. Rivulets tumble between the trees and views widen until lost below in thin cloud; monkeys chatter and scamper along the parapet; vultures and buzzards float overhead. Betty is happy. So am I.

The driver turns off the highway on to a side road in late afternoon and finally down a mud track. The guest house snuggles in a delightful woodland dell. It is a wooden building with dormer windows on the upper floor and a pleasant verandah. The tin roof could do with a paint and whoever accepted our reservations has forgotten to inform the staff.

Tattoos on the Ambassador's klaxon finally produce an elderly and clearly suspicious watchman.

Our driver talks Hindi both to the watchman and to his mobile.

The watchman scratches his already thinning hair before retreating to a shack at the rear of the guest house. He reappears with keys and somewhat reluctantly opens the front door. A large wooden table and chairs furnish the centre room, an en-suite bedroom on each side, two further bedrooms upstairs. Beds are narrow and unmade below furled and knotted mosquito nets. Naked electric bulbs are the fashion.

A short plump breathless gentleman in moderately clean khaki huffs and puffs down the track. 'Sorry,' he gasps. 'So sorry, sirs. No one is informing…'

Next to appear is an ancient and skeletal sweeper. The sweeper sweeps, a healthier and younger man arrives to make up the beds.

We enquire of the jeep that is part of our pre-paid package.

'Coming, sirs. Coming instantly…'

Our driver, assured of our safety, departs with promises to return the following afternoon. We sit on the verandah and sip tea produced from a kitchen that must be at the rear. Better it remain unseen. And feeding us is a problem; no money has been sent to buy provisions.

Betty and the manager depart on foot for a village a short distance up the road.

'Very close, sirs…'

I remain on the verandahh, continue sipping tea, and muse on Betty's possible reaction to being a sir.

An Indian version of the US army jeep arrives minus its canvas top. Left front wing is battered, otherwise reasonable and a vast improvement on a self-drive Jeep Betty and I hired in the Philippines. The original motor and gearbox on the Philippine jeep had been replaced. The replacement was smaller, less thirsty and less powerful. First gear was a failure climbing steep hills. The only way up was in reverse. Passengers walked.

Betty returns with the manager. The manager carries a very small live chicken, half a dozen potatoes in a string bag and a bundle of green leaves, plant unknown.

The sweeper has swept the dust back and forth. The bed-maker has made up the beds and unfurled the mosquito nets. Dusk is falling fast. Electricity is off. Betty and I choose rooms by torch light. Showers boast electric suicide heaters above the shower rose. Cold showers would have been refreshing down on the coast. Up in the hills cold is cold.

Thanks be to God (or Dutch intelligence), Betty has brought a bottle in memory of our Cuban adventures. The manager produces limes, a brown paper bag of slightly grubby sugar and a few sprigs of mint. Pleasant smells drift from the kitchen shack. Life improves.

The manager suggests we look for animals while waiting for dinner. Betty and I sit on heaped cushions in the back of the jeep. The manager sits beside the driver. He is armed with a large spotlight powered by wires from the jeep's battery. The beam sweeps the road edge and pries in between the trees. Twice we see eyes shinning – very exciting! And illegal, according to the manager, a special favour to console us for his lack of preparation.

'Now is dry season, sirs. Not much tourists coming…'

Dinner is edible. The mosquito nets have holes. The scent of freshly roasting coffee beans is a good awakening from a hellish night. The coffee is surprisingly good. So are the masala omelettes. We pack. The jeep delivers us to the offices of the wildlife sanctuary where a fat man behind a desk declares that private transport is forbidden. An elderly bus awaits us. Payment is requested for the bus, the bus driver and for a park ranger. Anger excites joy in the hearts of Indian officialdom. Saintly smiles are the only revenge; remain calm, smile and pay…

The park ranger directs the bus driver down dirt tracks. We sit on hard seats and gaze through dirty glass at a parched and sparse forest dressed in multiple shades of grey. Deer are plentiful, monkeys, wild pig, even a small herd of elephant in the distance. Betty is happy as she clicks away.

Bump goes the bus, bump bump bump, more deer, more pig, more monkeys. Betty deserves more. More isn't available. Tiger-hunting isn't what it was in the days of the Raj – or not in Kerala.

Our chauffeur and cream Ambassador awaits at the administrative building. The chauffeur recompenses us with lesser roads before plunging down to the littoral, coffee plantations thickly sprinkled with white blossom, villages for Betty to photograph, a few small temples, a shrine or two.

Kochi Fort has become familiar territory. Betty delights in searching the narrow streets and alleys for photo opportunities. We explore

Jew Town, visit the sixteenth-century synagogue fast surrendering to tourism, cross by ferry to Ernakulam for delicious food. Joyful is a day cruising canals in a narrow boat powered by a small diesel engine.

The shikari boat is furnished with two low couches deep with cushions and shaded by a frilled awning. The larger lagoons have become a cruising ground for houseboats. Trees drape the narrower waterways with shade. Cottages cluster along the towpaths where freshly washed cooking pots dry on the grass. Boys splash and chase each other. Girls, post-puberty, bathe fully dressed. Women bathe decorously. The vibrant green of paddy fields spreads beyond. Lunch is fresh fish grilled on charcoal followed by a perfect siesta on the piled cushions. Late afternoon and houseboats moor bow-to-stern against the banks of the bigger canals. The houseboats discharge human effluent into the canals. Once-beloved Kerala, why did you sell your charm? By what right do I complain of change? Be gone, old man. Scurry south with your ancient memories.

I have been riding these past weeks the warm, lush, multi-rivered littoral at the foot of the forested ghats. The southern stretch of this Indian odyssey finishes today at Kanyakumari, the subcontinent's southernmost point. Pick the exact spot and you can paddle with one foot in the Bay of Bengal, one in the Arabian Sea. Judging the exact spot once demanded a dozen priests of various faiths, a necromancer or two and at least one oracle. Now tourists consult their iPads, a further death to romance…

Distance from Kochi is three hundred kilometres on a good road. I leave early, book into a hotel and make for the beach an hour before sunset. Tens of thousands of Hindu pilgrims visit Kanyakumari each year to celebrate the rising of the sun. I am as happy photographing the sun sink into the ocean. A smooth boulder makes a good seat while waiting and cogitating on Kanyakumari's two architectural witnesses to religious faith: the Hindu temple is dedicated to the virgin goddess Kumari, the Catholic church to the Blessed Virgin.

The sun slips silently below the horizon. I head up to the church. Three tall Gothic towers dominate the small flagged square directly above the shore. The interior is bare of ornament. Mass has already started. God won't mind that I am a little late…

The hotel porter wakes me a half-hour before dawn. I climb the stairs to the flat roof. No Hindu chant greets me, rather a recorded sung Mass broadcast from the Catholic church. A woman sits on one of two plastic chairs and cradles a young girl on her lap. Her husband and another man clamber up a ladder to the hotel's water tower. The rungs are steel pipe. A large blister burst yesterday on the ball of my left foot. It hurts. I am wearing shoes, no socks. I haven't tied the laces (nor have I combed my hair and my teeth are in a mug in my bedroom). Which will be more painful: stooping to tie my laces or climbing the ladder on bare feet?

Or not climb the ladder?

Such are the quandaries of old men.

The mother with the child points to the spare plastic chair. Does she judge me too old for the ladder? Me, the Hells Angel of septuagenarians? I'll show her. Off come the shoes and up. The eastern sky is faintly tinged with orange. Behind us the moon hangs over a hotel. The hotel's roof is crowded with sunrise celebrants. So are all the roofs. Either my fellow guests at this hotel are lazy or have taken the true believers' route to the seashore. The sun rises. It is low-key rather than spectacular. I take photographs and return to my bed. The night porter offers me coffee or tea. They will taste much the same. That's OK. Dawn is done. Pilgrim buses are pulling out of town. It's going to be a great day…

9

NORTH TO KOLKATA

Kolkata is 2,400 kilometres north of Kanyakumari. That is a fair distance on a 125cc, five days' hard riding. I can't do hard riding any more. I've been away from home three and a half months; I'm tired.

For most travellers Madurai would be the first stop, 270 kilometres on National Highway 7. The land is dry when compared with the west. Wind generators replace the great trees of the western littoral and spread for miles left and right of the highway. Wind generators are splendid in their place – I recall a day exploring the heights of Spain's Sierra Maestrazgo. Guarding the jagged crest stood a line of majestic metal giants, their arms slowly turning against the deep blue of the sky. Don Quixote would have been delighted.

Such grandeur is sadly absent in a vast wind farm on flat dusty fields. However, one memory awakens another, now of Madurai so magical on that last journey 40 years ago. Of Hindu cities, Madurai is one of the most sacred. The Teppam Festival draws pilgrims in their tens of thousands to escort Shiva and his triple-breasted consort from the temple to the Mariamman Teppakulam tank.

Vanessa and I drove into town on the eve of the festival and met a young Brahman outside the temple. His father was the director of the festival. Thus we found ourselves on the float amongst the notables, two small pale-skinned figures seated at the feet of the gods, we utterly unimportant, yet permitted to share in the sacred. I remember the glow of the full moon and the ropes connecting the float to thousands of faces glistening in candlelight on the bank, and I remember the music, the drumming of the old master and the young master playing in turn, not in competition but lifting each other to an ever higher plane and we were lifted, transported. All of us. Oh yes, magic…

Dawn was only an hour away as we drove out of town. We turned off the highway a mile down a country road and unrolled the mattress beneath a neem tree. Now I pull in off the highway and remove my helmet to release the pain. If I could, I would run, anything to escape. No hiding from who I am nor from the sun that, at midday, dries the tears as I weep for a lost time, a lost chance to be a better person. Singing loudly drives the thoughts out. I recall few songs; bellowing 'Speed bonny boat like a bird on the wing' or 'I'll see a stranger across a crowded room' at a field of windmills is a little daft.

Surely I learned my lesson in Goa. Treasure your memories, learn from them, but move on. Better take the bypass round Madurai...

India does weird things to a traveller. It as easily fills you with loathing as lifts you with its magic. The road to Madurai took me into a dark place. A sign pointing off National Highway 7 to Kodaikanal is my escape route to unshared territory. The road approaches forested mountains across a flat fertile land of small paddy, coconut plantations and clean villages. I stop at a tiny café for tea and a small slice of cake. Four young men are my fellow customers. One of the men quizzes his companions for sufficient words with which to attempt communication beyond a smile. Hi, is all they manage. I can do Hi. To the reader, a single syllable must seem inadequate. Not to the traveller. The intention counts, offering of friendship, the desire to learn something of each other. Such is happiness.

Kodaikanal is 2,300 metres above sea level. The settlement was founded in 1834 by US missionaries as a shelter from the fierce heat and diseases of the plain. Kodai remains healthy – almost no mosquitoes. The missionaries built a sanatorium and a school. The school continues.

A good road winds up the mountains through thick forest. Waters of Vaigai Lake sparkle in the valley below. Young rice is harlequin-green amongst the darker palm and banana plantations. In the background rise the Varushanad Hills.

Signs warn drivers and riders to sound their horns. I obey. Two young men on a bike wave me down and point uphill into the forest. I sit on the stone parapet and watch bison graze amongst the trees. The undergrowth allows only brief glimpses of a calf. The calf is paler than the adults. What pleasure in breathing cool, forest-scented air. And so upward, the late afternoon chill on my chest and I wonder whether to stop and drag out the sweater from my backpack.

Kodai has three centres: the bazaar, the star-shaped 24-hectare lake and the International School. The J Heritage Hotel is at the head of a lane leading to the bazaar. Wealthy travellers should beware; the J Heritage Hotel is not a Heritage Hotel. Nor is it a dump. Or not quite. It is of wood construction. It is better viewed through half-closed eyes. Add imagination and optimism and it could claim a modicum of charm. And it is cheap, or cheap by Kodaikanal rates, which are high as they are in all hill stations. Hill stations are for the privileged: provincial governors, judges, senior military, civil servants of collector rank and above. Servants are the norm. Visitors have energy and time to row on the lake, jog, ride bikes, ride horses and walk the many paths. Such voluntary exercise fosters a good healthy sweat; sweat is involuntary down on the plains. Surely a curious division between the elite and the hoi polloi…

So far on this journey I have conversed either with other foreigners or with the middle-aged and older. I long for young voices. I am in Kodaikanal for the International School.

The school is co-educational. Sixty per cent of the 571 students are Indian nationals, 121 are from other Asian countries, 58 North American, 41 from Europe, 7 African, a lone New Zealander and a lone Omani. The curriculum melds the US public school syllabus with the international baccalaureate. One hundred per cent progress to university, not a bad record… And the school has 14 music teachers.

In earlier days the school produced diplomats, administrators and academics. The modern trend is towards entrepreneurs and CEOs.

My own opinion? A joyful and stimulating path to adulthood…

Put most of Asia in a cocktail shaker, add a smidgen of Irish and unlimited enthusiasm and you have the school's vice principal. I've omitted intellectual curiosity and intellectual discipline of which he has ample, and my joy at discovering that he is a historian.

He is similar to President Obama in thinking before replying to a question – a habit that is politically disastrous according to the professor of Sanskrit (University of Pennsylvania) whom I met on the road south. The US voter demands immediate replies. Pause for thought shows indecisiveness. It also leads to confusion as shown when a woman staff member telephones the vice principal with my request for an interview and pre-empts his answer with a firm negative – wrongly as it happens. Unravelling the confusion takes a while and I am in Kodaikanal two days before I meet the vice principal and a further day to gain permission to sit in on a class of final year students.

The students are discussing manipulation of thought through maps, photography and metaphor. Am I prejudiced in finding the girls intellectually more mature?

The class finishes and I remain at table with three students – two girls and a boy. They are fresh-faced 17-year-olds. The boy and one of the girls are Indian. The second girl is the daughter of Europeans in the missionary/aid sector and long resident in India. Teenagers tend to be wary of revealing themselves. They find safety in numbers. A full class and I might be able to provoke a general discussion – even an argument. Three is too few – though I try with the question I posed throughout Hispanic America: Why do so few students intend entering public service?

Student 1 (female Indian): Pay is too low.

Student 2 (female European born and raised in India): It is the fault of modern Indian society. Everyone for themselves.

Student 3 (male Indian) has no opinion. He wants to be a sports journalist.

Are none of them tempted to enter politics?

Student 1 (female Indian) says that it is impossible to remain clean in Indian politics – a view shared by the other two.

End of subject.

Do they spend much time in their imagination?

Student 3 (male Indian) imagines doing things – driving a fast car, scoring a goal.

Student 1 (female Indian) fears that she spends too much time in her imagination, that it affects her grades.

I want to ask, not what she dreams, but why she dreams. Is she seeking shelter and from what?

From whom she thinks she is?

Or from what is expected of her?

Or from what she expects?

I don't have the right and Student 2 (female European) is talking now of a lonely childhood in which her only companions were imaginary – as they were mine both as a child and as a writer of fiction.

My thanks to these young for sharing time. I will be gone in the morning.

The road north from Kodaikanal to Panali is a narrow serpent of tar twisting down through broad-leaf forest. This is a road to be taken slowly, each corner relished; to delight in the shifting sunlight filtered through tree-cover, inhale the moist freshness of earth scent, catch glimpses of a river curling across flat fields spread below.

The rise in temperature from Kodaikanal down to Panali is 20 degrees. No need for the leather bomber jacket after the first half-hour. The jumper is next to go. Panali onward to Tiruchirappalli is a further two and a half hours – enough for this old man.

Tiruchirappalli is the second largest of Tamil Nadu's cities. An impressive sixteenth-century temple fortress commands the city from the crest of a mammoth chunk of rock. Beyond flows one of India's longest rivers, the Kaveri or Cauvery, once a major transport link between coast and hills. Room rate with air conditioning at a good modern hotel in the Cantonment area is less than Kodai's J Heritage.

The ride onward to the beach town of Mamallapuram should be

easy; stupidly I left that essential of Indian road travel, the Eicher road atlas, in the lobby of the J Heritage Hotel.

I either imagine that Mamallapuram is north of Chennai or don't think. I have bypassed Chennai and am heading for Kolkata before realising my error. This is a hot day. Riding through the city is energy-sapping and Chennai traffic is fearful. All locals from whom I ask directions have difficulty in differentiating left from right. A bus labelled as heading for Mamallapuram is my saviour. I follow out to the coast road.

My memories of Mamallapuram are of a small village on a dirt track, shore temples and sculpture, a few fishing boats dragged up on the sand and not much else. Modern Mamallapuram is crammed with foreign tourists, tourist touts and day-trippers. *Lonely Planet* recommends Tina's Lodge. The proprietor shows me a single room down a dank dark corridor. Were it a jail cell, prisoners would complain justifiably to the International Court of Human Rights. The so-called bathroom? Ugh! A young Israeli woman in a marginally better room laughs at the speed of my retreat. The manager assures me that a better room will be available tomorrow. The better room has a terrace that the breeze can't reach. I peer through the open door at a heat-haggard tourist sweating on the bed, remount and go exploring.

The Sunrise Guest House isn't listed in the guidebooks. New-build, it is too distant from the main tourist strip for researchers to walk on a hot day. I am offered a room three times the size of the Tina prison cell. Both room and bathroom are spotless. Wall-to-wall windows face the park and the sea. Open the windows and a splendid sea breeze lifts the curtains – same daily rate as the hellhole cell and with satellite TV. Climb stairs to the thatch-roof restaurant and I can plug the laptop into a power point. Fried rice with calamari is good. Such is perfection.

I have drunk only one small cup of coffee this morning and my thoughts remain somewhat disorganised. The plains of Tamil Nadu in March are hot. Fortunately a strong breeze cools the roof terrace of the Sunrise Guest House in Mamallapuram. A grass park and a few palm trees separate the guest house from the sea. The sea is a pale green-blue beneath a sky that is paler than pale. Surf breaks on the rock shore. Two small, narrow, high-bowed fishing boats rock at anchor. Four sister boats have chugged south down the coast. The elderly cook is preparing fresh coffee. Ten minutes and my brain will be unscrambled. I will write.

Determination to bring the writing up to date has kept me yoyoing for five days between a table on the rooftop terrace and an inter-net café. Vanessa keeps entering my thoughts. The grass park below stretches some three hundred metres to the sea. Vanessa and I camped in the grove of palm trees to the right of the park. The shore temples were unique, caves carved out of the rock, gods sculpted out of the rock.

We sat one morning on a stone ledge at the back of a temple cave and contemplated the god. Which god I don't recall. A truck braked outside the cave. Four Japanese entered and set up lights and lighting screens and three canvas chairs, one of which had DIRECTOR written in large square letters on the back. The director arrived in a white Morris Ambassador. The Japanese filmed the god and left without once acknowledging our existence.

I recall strolling the beach hand in hand another morning and so much seemed tantalisingly familiar. The gods, seen with peripheral vision, flickered an entirety of sculptural history, or so it seemed, Ancient Greece, Michelangelo, Giacometti.

Now stone walls protect caves and temples against future tsuna-mis. Buy a ticket to enter.

News has spread of an old Brit revisiting after 40 years. The owner of the guest house brings an elderly fisherman up to the terrace. The fisherman claims to remember Vanessa's and my previous visit. He describes the Volkswagen, points a gnarled finger at the palm trees where we camped and says that he brought us fish each morning and each evening. The guest house cook brings fresh coffee and we sit at the table and share our memories. There wasn't even a bus service, recalls the fisherman. I remember a cool sea breeze after swimming and that we built a fire and grilled the fish over the embers. The owner of the guest house would have been in nappies.

Chennai was Madras in the 1970s. I bumped a woman with the front wing as we drove through a village. I had read newspaper reports of drivers stoned to death after an accident. Never stop was the repeated warning. The hood was down on the VW. Vanessa was with me. No way would I stop. A white Ambassador chased us, men armed with sticks leaning out of the windows. I took to rough dirt roads, the VW faster over the bumps and ruts. Fifteen minutes and we'd lost the pursuit. In Madras, we booked into a hotel before driving to the central police station. A superintendent interviewed us in his office. I confessed to a hit and run.

The superintendent said that stopping would have been irresponsible. The woman had been brought to the police station. She wasn't hurt. Any offer of money would be taken as an admission of guilt. A lawyer would tie me up with a civil case. I'd be in Madras for months.

Today I am riding to Chennai from Mamallapuram at the behest of *Motorcycle News*. The editor I deal with has suggested a piece on the Royal Enfield factory. Royal Enfield is the last relic of the British motorcycle industry. The first motorcycle was produced at a factory in Redditch, Worcestershire, in 1901. The Chennai factory opened in 1955 to fulfil an Indian government order for 800 350cc Bullets. The British factory closed in 1967. Chennai prospers under the financial umbrella of the Eicher truck company. Manufacturing process competes with the bikes for antiquity in an immense tin shed with open eaves. Bikes are assembled by hand, no robots here. Prior to mounting in the chassis, an aged elf equipped with headphones and stethoscope runs each motor in a tiny cubicle. The paint shop is a paint mist; two men in overalls and masks are visible through a window as they spray-paint the gas tanks. A true artist adds in free-hand the golden line on the tanks. Each bike is test ridden round the cinder track that surrounds the factory.

Priority for any long-distance traveller is comfort and I bounce-test each model: 350cc and 500, military, classic, the new low rider, single seat and dual. My favourite? The big broad single saddle mounted on coil springs.

I rode a BSA Bantam in the early fifties. Cops were called Bobbies and patrolled on silent water-cooled Velocettes. Vincents were power with speed. Sunbeams were deluxe touring. AJS, Norton, all deceased and gone to Heaven. Royal Enfield in Redditch was a casualty. What miracle saved Royal Enfield here in Chennai?

'Why buy an Enfield?' is a reasonable question to ask the market-ing manager over lunch.

His reply is as offbeat as hand-spraying gas tanks: There's no logical reason. Enfields are heavy. They're slow. They're not fuel-efficient.

'India's hog,' I suggest.

The marketing manager disagrees: In whatever company, Harleys always dominate. The Bullet becomes part of wherever it is.

I argue that the originals were British as fish and chips, the Bullet is now quintessentially Indian. Bullet Super Strong is India's most lethal beer. A temple in Rajasthan is dedicated to a Bullet. Remove the bike from the temple and it will be back by sunrise – so they say.

'So it is romantic,' I insist. 'The Morgan of the bike world.'

Again the marketing manager demurs: Morgans are high-price status symbols. Bullets are workhorses.

A horse rider feels the muscles bunch and flow and listens to the rhythm of the horse's breathing. The rider of the Bullet feels the beat of the engine and the slow glorious thump of the exhaust. Such is the Bullet's magic.

The marketing manager will disagree. Magic has no place in his vocabulary – strange, as he is so obviously a romantic.

My final conclusion: Enfields look and sound as a bike should. This, of course, is the opinion of a biker born before the war. I hear my four sons chant in unison, 'Which war, Dad? The Boer War?' Not kind, but I'm accustomed to put-downs from the young.

Back in Mamallapuram, I chat with a young Indian couple in an internet café during one of many power cuts. University students, they share a hotel room. Does this make them liberals or is room-sharing common amongst the young educated in India? Or is it a class thing? Asking would be impolite.

Their dress is India's equivalent of Gap; English is their language at home – though she doesn't talk much (embarrassed?), while he is vocal and definite in his opinions. His father is a senior military officer. The student believes India has a great future. Central government is building new power stations in every state. Power cuts will be history.

And salaries in India are the fastest rising worldwide; the brain drain to the US will stop.

Corruption is the greatest problem. Corruption amongst politicians is endemic. *We must change everything.* He doesn't know how. Neither he nor any of his friends vote. They aren't interested in politics. However change will come from the people. The people vote.

But not students? Surely a little weird...

A German couple, mid-thirties, tall, fair-haired and tanned, arrive at the Sunrise Guest House from an ashram on the Holy Mountain. He does the talking (perhaps his father is a senior military officer). Merely breathing the same air as the Maharishi was an uplifting and joyous experience. No need for talk. Or for teaching. The Maharishi's presence was sufficient. Mostly they meditated; surely a suitable holiday for a designer of state-of-the-art aircraft seats. He presumes that I must know which Holy Mountain and which Maharishi. Disabusing him would be unkind. He is a vegetarian. They run a vegetarian household. She has steak when they eat out and teaches handicapped children. I suspect that she hopes for more than meditation in the future.

I have been lying in bed and thinking, not of myself but of Vanessa. How would she judge me, so maudlin in my memories? Too much has changed. Mamallapuram was our private paradise. It has become one more grubby outpost of *Lonely Planet* land. I am jealous of the young, of their sharing what was ours. And, yes, I am critical of their conduct. Not all, of course, but many. Of their slovenly adoption of Indian clothes. Or, more accurately, the Indian clothes they chose to wear. A strange mixture, never quite clean.

I remember a dinner party at Amin's parents' home on the point above Pajim. Amin's mother and I were the only non-Goans. The hippy colony on Calangute was under discussion.

'Why must they wear our clothes?' came from a lady in an off-the-shoulder evening dress.

The 'our clothes' rankled. 'Our clothes' indeed, with every woman in evening dress; amongst the men, I was alone in not wearing a dinner jacket.

I did wear Indian clothes, not on the road, but in Mumbai during the heat of summer. An image comes of the great dining room of the Taj, the maître d'hotel conducting me to a table where my host is already seated. My dress is a spotless white kurta and pyjamas fresh from the laundry, both top and bottom starched and ironed crisp as a sheet of quality writing paper.

No, there was nothing slovenly in my appearance – my host was one of the two Tata brothers who then controlled the Tata empire.

The contempt I read for today's Western young offends me, not that Indians are contemptuous of them but that the young don't notice or don't care. I think of it as the Benidorm syndrome. Drunken holidaymakers spewing in the street, language obscene. No sense of pride, or of dignity. So there you have it, the Old Blimp grumbling into his beard.

Time to move on, to somehow escape the tourist route, experience fresh territory. The North East states beckon: Darjeeling, Assam, Sikkim, perhaps Nagaland (if the road is open and travel permits obtainable).

Bypassing Chennai takes three hours, then up National Highway 5, dual carriageway and a good surface with the usual crop of crashed trucks, countryside flat, harvested paddy fields sun-baked, soil dead in the heat. Stop for a moment and sweat soaks my shirt. The Honda alone seems impervious to the heat and cruises happily at 80 kph. I manage 420 kilometres to the city of Vijayawada on the Krishna River and find a reasonable hotel.

It will be another hot day. Leave early for the coolness and you witness the night's disasters before they are towed away. Today's worst is an overturned truck with another truck embedded in it. The driver was heading the wrong way down the dual carriageway. Exactly how the crash happened, I don't know. I'm an observer rather than a specialist. Photographing the mashed cabs would be unfeeling.

And I am forced off the road in the space of an hour by two buses heading right at me as they overtake other vehicles. This is all before my first stop for tea and a breakfast dosa. I've had enough. To hell with this. I'm heading for the Himalayas. Maybe mountain people are more considerate.

Another day northward across the same flat countryside from Andhra Pradesh into Orissa. Orissa is poor. Frighteningly poor. Depressing. *The Times of India* carries a report of 75 government paramilitary killed in a Naxalite ambush. Naxalites are India's Maoists. They have been conducting a low-level clandestine war for the past 40 years. Action centres on the rural areas of Orissa and Bihar. Rural poverty is the catalyst.

National Highway 5 is being widened. Dirt deviations bypass bridges and culverts under construction. Logjam follows logjam as truck and bus drivers jostle senselessly for non-existent space. The set-up on the Stunner is more pain-giving on bad roads than the Cargo I rode through the Americas. The seat angle throws the rider's weight forward on to his hands and I end a 10-hour day at Srikakulam with bruised palms and a pain in the butt. The hotel is overpriced at 650 rupees. A dosa for dinner at a workman's café costs 20 rupees. I set the kilometre trip to zero this morning. It registers 522, good going for an oldie in his dotage.

Pimples on the butt are the inevitable result of hours sweating on a bike seat. Germolene stops infection. 520 kilometres yesterday was too much. How do I feel this morning? Wrecked.

I am on the road by 7 a.m. and have breakfast at a truck driver's stop. The owner was a Customs officer at Delhi airport for 12 years and speaks English. Where am I from? Where am I going? How long have I been on the road? When will I go home? Am I married? Children? Grandchildren? Truck drivers listen as he translates my answers.

My turn with questions. A driver's wages?

Between eight and 10 thousand rupees monthly depending on the hours they drive. Mostly they drive at night – less traffic and the engines don't overheat. The ex-Customs officer adds that drivers take pills to keep awake.

Back on the road and the heat hits. The highway passes inland of a vast lagoon, the air thick with salt scent. Pull into a gas station, no breeze and I'm sweat-drenched in seconds. This is a tough day. I check my replacement Eicher road atlas, a gift from Royal Enfield marketing. The beach town of Puri is the day's goal. I will have ridden 260 kilometres – not far for a day's run but all that I can sensibly manage.

Most visitors travel to Puri via the state capital. I take a short cut down a single-track country road from the south-west. The first five kilometres are good tar. For the next 15 I creep between elephant traps and moguls of baked mud. But what a glorious countryside of straw-cottage villages, temple ponds shaded by giant peepal trees and baobabs, emerald paddy studded with coconut palms. I bump and bounce past a truck. A bridge crosses a creek sheeted with hyacinth and water lily. Buffalo bask with only their noses above the surface.

A stop to photograph a basket market; pull in at a tin-shack canteen for a cold soda. The owner has been playing cricket.

The revered Jagannath Temple attracts tens of thousands of Hindu pilgrims to Puri. A great beach and relaxed attitude to bhang was the original attraction for backpackers. A rash of hotels and restaurants result. In a previous life the Z Hotel was a Maharajah's beach house. The manager is vague as to which Maharajah. My room is marginally smaller than a squash court. The cloud island in the middle is a four-poster bed with mosquito net. A fan turns slowly above the net. Open all the windows and the net billows in the breeze. For furniture there is a desk, one easy chair, two upright chairs, a wardrobe and a wooden clothes rack. Crossing the bathroom is a major expedition – pack sandwiches. All this for 750 rupees. Not such a tough life…

Back to bed only to be disturbed by an uncomfortable thought: the painter, Constable, marketed a fine line of rural romantic poverty. I've been uploading photographs of thatched one-room cottages taken on the side road to Puri. Guilt? Definitely…

I share a bowl of fruit salad and curd with a placidly beautiful Chinese woman whose age I underestimate by 10 years. She is trying to find herself. More fruit salad and she corrects herself: she has a low boredom threshold and is searching either for an occupation that will hold her interest or for the discipline to resist moving on at the first yawn.

In part, her problem is a fast, well-trained mind (my opinion). She is a graduate of the London School of Economics.

I suggest day trading as an adrenalin rush. She did that for 10 years. It became obsessive, one more computer game.

Writing appeals to her – though she doubts her staying power.

I suggest a fake autobiography: Chinese high-flier drops a million in the morning and makes her dinner date suffer. Have you done that?

Yes, maybe…

Which is a definite affirmative in any language.

And she doubts whether she could satisfy the US/UK chick lit market. Chinese women have a perception of romance more subtle that the Western sob and groan version, so she claims. The perfect husband is perfectly manipulable…

We will meet again tomorrow for more fruit salad. Aged 40, she is a year or two younger than my friend, Ming, with whom I travelled through Ecuador and Peru. They share a splendid Chinese elitism.

Four thousand years of bad ceramics was Ming's critique of pre-Colombian art. My present companion dismisses the London School of Economics as one more brand name along with Gucci, Prada and Louis Vuitton.

Eight guests for dinner are thinly spread at the Z Hotel's single dining table. The table seats 40. Perhaps it is a remnant of the long-gone Maharajah's splendour. A young couple from Penn State are in management with a VSO program further south. The previous volunteer left six months prior to their arrival. No trace remains of this volunteer's work – work that these two are now duplicating. Little wonder that they are increasingly cynical. They will be in India for two years. They came with hopes of achieving something for the poor. Their cynicism worries them. They admire Obama and fear that he will be a one-term president. They talk of his race speech during the primaries as a turning point in the election. They talk of their pride as they listened to the speech, proud to bear witness to the good side of America.

A portly Canadian in his sixties and looking older wonders whether he should buy a diamond from a pedlar on the beach. The unanimous opinion offered by his fellow guests at the Z Hotel is an instant negative. He, however, is determined that he has found a bargain. He bought a stone in Rajasthan some years back for US $1,000. The gem dealer assured him that it had a value of $2,000. Back home a jeweller confirmed the value at $2,000. This, of course, was the price a jeweller would sell rather than the price at which a jeweller would buy the stone. The Canadian eventually sold the stone for US $600 yet believes that he made a profit.

Perhaps he should try baskets…

Breakfast and the elderly overweight Canadian remains undecided as to beach diamonds. He has a further concern. Leather belts are a tenth the price of belts back home in Canada. Should he buy belts with the standard buckle or in the modern flip-over style?

I gave up wearing belts on my fiftieth birthday. I wear what we Brits call braces and the Americans call suspenders. I wear them outside my shirt. The Canadian is clearly asking advice of the wrong person. This doesn't stop him.

I walk the beach, struggle through a few thousand pilgrims to admire the temple, eat curd and fruit salad with my Chinese lady friend (she leaves for Darjeeling tomorrow) and avoid further discussions of belts and diamonds. Tomorrow I head north towards Kolkata.

I got hit by a bus today. Not me personally, but the right-side wing mirror. I was riding through a small town on a typical Indian main street: buses, trucks, tractors dragging trailers, rickshaws, bikes and pedal bicyclists, loaded handcarts, cows, a few goats, hundreds of pedestrians. The bus overtook me where there was no room. It shoved me off the road on to soft dirt. I was fortunate to miss a couple of pedestrians and a handcart. I passed a bad smash a few kilometres later out in the country. A rickshaw had pulled out in front of a speeding biker, a young guy, no helmet. The bike was on its side in the road. The biker lay on the grass verge. His head was all blood and he wasn't moving. A crowd had gathered, gawpers. Presumably they were waiting for or hoping for an ambulance.

The ride north is tough, not simply the distance and the traffic, but the heat. Perhaps I have been aiming for too long a daily distance. Or age is overtaking my ambitions. Whatever, I remain tired despite the break at Puri. Kolkata is a further 500 kilometres. I stop midway at a small fishing village, Chandipur. A clean air-conditioned room with a reasonable mattress is 650 rupees at the Hotel Shubhan. I planned a swim before dinner. The tide is out; out at Chandipur is five kilometres. I return to the hotel, apply a coating of Deet, sit out on the terrace and enjoy the evening breeze. Deet is miraculous. In four months of travel I've been bitten at most half a dozen times. I should write. I prefer meditating on the fresh crab the hotel manager has promised for dinner. Chandipur is famous for crab – crab and the five-kilometre tide. The power cuts when I am on the stairs down to the restaurant. No problem. Obligatory evening wear for India includes a mini Leatherman flashlight. Up-end the flashlight on the table and the light bounces back off the ceiling.

I am criticised often for being too political in my writing and having an anti-American agenda. These critics mean the USA rather than America in general and US foreign policy in particular. Now I have a new critic, who posted on Amazon the following criticism of *Old Man on a Bike*. *I bought this for my husband at his request. He was fired with enthusiasm from an article he read in the* Telegraph. *He is totally disappointed in this book and literally had to struggle through it. He sums it up as a description of breakfast in many places. It is therefore not recommended.*

For those readers who don't care for breakfast, be warned…

Breakfast in Chandipur is a masala crab omelette.

Kolkata on the map looks an easy ride. Side roads are a mistake. Directions given by the hotel manager at Chandipur were somewhat vague and difficulties arise on entering any big city. Signposts either abandon you midway through the suburbs or, worse, point in a direction that doesn't correspond with the six exits on a major intersection.

OK, so it's a left, but which left? The first? Or the second?

Hesitate a millisecond and three hundred enraged drivers hit their klaxons.

I complained once to a dive companion that he didn't understand how frightened I was when a dive became difficult, or even threatened to become difficult. I'm a coward, I insisted.

He argued that I merely had an unusually strong sense of self-preservation.

He was wrong.

I am a coward, particularly if threatened with an emotional confrontation.

Or when an unsilenced heavy machine gun fires a burst directly under my butt: *tacka tacka tacka*.

HELP!

I slow and the rate of fire slows.

I speed up, the rate of fire increases.

I pull in to the kerb and the firing stops.

I am riding a Honda 125. Honda 125s never break down. This article of faith supported me on my exploration of the Americas – 66,000 kilometres. It has supported me on this journey through India – 11,000 kilometres. Now fear hits. Real fear. Or belly-emptying anxiety (which is fear, surely?).

Tacka tacka tacka fires the machine gun as I creep into a gas station. Hell and damnation…

I come to a halt and rev the engine. No machine gun, so the engine is OK. It must be the gearbox. I dismount and heave the bike on to its stand. I look at the gearbox. My knowledge of gearboxes could be written on the point of a very, very thin needle and looking doesn't help. I touch the gearbox tentatively with a fingertip. Touching tells me nothing. I look at the two gas pump attendants. Surely one of them can wave a wand?

The smaller of the two grins and points at my rear wheel. An eight-inch nail sticks out of the tread. I put the bike into gear. The rear wheel spins. The nail strikes the rear mudguard: *tacka tacka tacka*…

I suffer from the sin of pride. Not always, but on occasion. Hey, I'm nearly 80 and look at me, *brrrm brrrm* on a café racer round India. Kneeling in the gas station forecourt is an act of humility. The pump attendants and a few drivers and bike riders watch as I waggle the eight-inch nail out of the tyre. The tyre is not punctured. Not so my pride… Such is the punishment for my momentary lack of faith. Remember, Old Man, Honda 125s never ever break down…

Pointless to ask directions to a one-star hotel unless you are close. Not so with the Taj Bengal (not so with any Taj Hotel). I stay at the Taj for two reasons. Firstly, the Taj Group invite me. Secondly, the Taj in Bombay was my security blanket 40 years ago. Entering the great dining room overlooking the sea was an instant antidote to depression or fatigue. I took personally the storming of the Taj by terrorists. They attacked treasured memories. Fear the terrorists and they have the victory. This ride is both my response and my inadequate memorial to the killed and to a dear and respected friend, sadly departed, Darab Tata.

Six guards protect the gates into the Taj Hotel, Kolkata. No entry for an Old Blimp on a Honda 125. Baby bikes are for servants. I park with the social pariahs and walk. Security at the lobby entrance is airport style. Place keys, small change, mobile phones, etc. in a wicker tray for X-ray scan. Pass through the detector gates. My braces set off the alarm. Take them off and I have to hold up my pants. Hardly a glorious entrance to five-star luxury…

I giggle. So do the security guards.

A suave gentleman in a frock coat betrays neither surprise nor dismay at spotting an aged tramp on wealth-hallowed ground. 'Mister Gandolfi?'

'Yes,' say I. Are they expecting another ancient scruff?

However great the number of rooms, the best hotels make each guest feel unique and treasured. Is it years of training or brilliant selection of staff? Probably an amalgam of both.

Taj staff are brilliant.

First goal? Soak in a hot bath… And soak and soak. Then sprawl on a perfect mattress and check my address book. Then connect the laptop to the Wi-Fi for mail.

Is Bernadette OK?

Has my suicidal last-born survived a further week of snowboarding?

What news of my other children and my grandchildren?

What work am I late delivering?

And what funds remain in the bank? This last is always a major anxiety on a long journey.

I sit on a sofa in an outer office on the top floor of a commercial building in central Kolkata. The invitation was for 7 p.m. to 7:30. It is now 8:30. I have read the *Times of India*, the *Hindu* and the *Statesman*. Sensible would have been to leave an hour ago. On the other hand the woman I expected to meet is my only contact here in Kolkata. I am told that she is rich, that she is interesting, that she does interesting things with her money. I am a writer. Interesting people are the grist for my writer's mill. The lady arrives at 8:45. She is short, plump, middle-aged and has steel chains woven into her hair. The chains reach midway down her thighs. Her desk is piled with pink purses encased in glass-bead spaniels. The curved doggy tail is the handle. Wow!

A guest swims lengths of the pool as I breakfast at a window table at the Taj Bengal. The latest BA *High Life* piece needs final editing. I am late with 1,500 words for a magazine. I must face the laptop keyboard. I occupy the same window table for a lunchtime meeting with the hotel's director of PR, Mrs Modhurima Sinha. Six tourists lounge on sunbeds the far side of the pool. I head back to my room, tap tap tap. Dinner is room service biryani and 30 minutes of IPL cricket live on TV. I call Bernadette at midnight and collapse into bed. Have I finished writing? Of course not.

Why do I write so slowly?

An immensely rich Kolkata businessman tells me of reneging on the purchase of a London hotel. His London lawyer, a man with Indian antecedents, warned him of disadvantages in doing business in England. Miss-declare trading figures for United Kingdom value added tax and you pay a fine. Do so a second time and you go to jail. India is different. Law is negotiable.

Mrs Modhurima Sinha wishes to introduce me to an old friend, Colonel Rajen Bali. She assures me that her friend and I will find much in common. We sit together in the lobby of the Taj Bengal. The colonel is the shorter by three inches and the younger by four years. He boasts a hawk's nose. Mine is snubbed. We are both overweight and bearded and we both served in the army, I as a lowly lieutenant. Rajen Bali has put his retirement to good use, both as a successful painter and one of India's foremost travel writers and writers on food. Mrs Modhurima Sinha probably sees us as grumpy old men and made for each other. So it proves…

Rajen Bali is married. His wife is away in Delhi visiting their only son. I am to occupy their spare room for the remainder of my stay in Kolkata. How do we pass our time? Talk endlessly of the past and of places visited and, disapprovingly, of the state of the world. Where has honour gone?

Elderly gentlemen, we quickly establish habits. Writing first, then breakfast, followed by more writing for which cold beer is the reward. Then lunch. But what a lunch…

The Balis are a Hindu warrior clan from the North West Frontier region of what is now Pakistan. Partition exiled them to India. Rajen was raised in Lucknow and served in the army through much of the border states and with the United Nations in the Congo. On retirement, he moved to Kolkata, primarily because he was unknown and wished to begin a new life. In doing so, he deliberately abandoned both his possessions and the privileges of rank – a clean sweep. Natives of Kolkata remain resident by habit. Rajen is an explorer. I benefit from his exploration.

Two Old Blimps are ready to party. Down the stairs we hobble and out on to the sidewalk. Rajen Bali swings both arms forward in time with his first few steps, swing and clap, swing and clap. It is a gesture common to minor public school games masters and First World War army commanders. 'Come on, chaps, up and at them.'

I am the only chap and I'm ready – though not speedy. Neither is Rajen Bali. An ankle smashed by three trucks in Tierra del Fuego slows me down. A freak wave did for the colonel's knee. We don't give a damn. We make a great pair.

First stop is always the Chhota Bristol, Kolkata's oldest bar and owned by the same family for four generations. The entrance off a side street is unobtrusive, no name on the door. Look for it and you won't find it. The owner wishes it to remain so. Publicity is anathema. Bring out a camera and you'd be ejected. The room is large, low-ceilinged, utilitarian and without decoration. Tables are marble-topped, the air conditioning works, and beer is only 10 per cent above retail price. The clientele range up and down the social scale from barrister to blue-collar bankrupt, judge to market trader, pensioner to youthful whippersnapper, no women allowed. One corner is a traditional haven for poets and writers hiding from their mothers-in-law. Quiet drinking and quiet conversation are expected. Drunks and loudmouths are banned. For us, one bottle is sufficient. We sit quietly, content in each other's company, and tell tales of what made us who we are.

'Boring,' my younger sons would say. Or, 'Heard that…'

True, perhaps, but what would they prefer? Silence?

An elderly gentleman at the next table has fallen asleep.

Travellers eat mediocre food much of the time. Ignorant of where to eat, we consult guidebooks or trust to chance. Writers of guidebooks are equally ignorant and chance is seldom the path to glory. Encyclopaedic knowledge of Kolkata makes Rajen Bali a brilliant pilot through the city's culinary highways and byways. His tastes are eclectic. Plush or plastic table is immaterial. Only the food counts. Kasturi on Mustaque Ahmed Street is the oldest Bengali restaurant in Kolkata. Climb stairs to a narrow room. Sit at a plastic-topped table, no menu, and eat fresh seafood. A waiter offers a dozen different dishes. I would be bewildered, nervous. Rajen selects. All are delicious. Salt-water prawn in a gently spiced sauce is extraordinary.

We sit in the proprietor's office after lunch. Rajen and the proprietor talk of cooking. Why no menu? Because dishes and prices change each day. The proprietor does the buying at the fish market. Quality and knowledge of what his customers can afford govern his choice.

Krazy Kebab is newly opened and designer modern – somewhere to take a business client. Westerners will find ordering easier than at Kasturi. The kebabs are good. Try the lamb chops, *Adrak ke panje*. They melt in your mouth. Or the chef's own invention: *Ghost Aftab*. And there is an excellent value lunchtime buffet. The chef in his whites and tall hat sits with us. He was an executive chef with the Taj Hotel Group. He left to build his own small empire. Good fortune to him.

Rajen has persuaded a businessman and his wife to breakfast with us at the Chinese street market: a young woman squats on the pavement; a 10-litre aluminium pot of chicken soup simmers over coals. The squatting stall holder rinses bowls in a bucket – sufficiently clean for the colonel and I. The businessman's wife has brought her own cup. Her husband talks on his mobile. Rajen discusses herbs and spices with the cook. Rajen remembers her mother – there are subtle differences in the daughter's stock. Beyond the stalls, women chop piles of salvaged timber into kindling. One feeds a baby at the breast. A tiny tot has picked up a hatchet. A family have roofed with cardboard a crack between two shacks; the mother washes two toddlers in the gutter. Our next stop, stuffed dumplings. The businessman's wife declines...

I love Kolkata. Communist state governments, unfriendly to business, have curtailed investment. One result: the city suffers from less industrial pollution than Delhi or Mumbai. A second plus: no arguments with cab drivers. Cabs have meters, drivers switch them on. Shopping in the markets is a pleasure. Stall holders are friendly. The language is musical. More English is spoken. I can communicate.

I explore the city while Rajen organises the final stages of my journey into Sikkim and the north-eastern states (warning: an

Inner Line Permit is necessary for those travelling to Sikkim). Few relics of the Mughals survive. Those of the British Raj have done better. The Writers Building (1780), headquarters of the East India Company, now houses the Government Secretariat. Built to impress the natives, the palatial Government House in sweeping pleasure gardens is home to the governor of West Bengal. The governor is a political appointee.

Mown and groomed is the great Park Street cemetery where immense trees shade the splendidly pretentious tombs of Britain's sahibs. The Scottish servants of empire buried their dead apart in a six-acre cemetery off Karaya Bazaar Road: the cemetery is a disaster zone, every grave vandalised, tombs stripped of their marble – surely a warning against independence.

This is my third journey as a septuagenarian. The true adventure is in the mind. Mount the saddle and, day after day, the same thoughts await. The Iraq War and its aftermath obsessed me as I rode through the Americas. The vileness of Abu Ghraib filled the airwaves, yet none of my fellow countrymen had resigned. Was honour outdated? Acceptance of responsibility superseded by desire for a larger pension pot…?

On this journey a fresh obsession was born as I watched Muslim women shopping in the outdoor market in Murud. This was a day, hot and humid, for the lightest of clothes; the women were cloaked head to foot in black.

What happens in India is for Indians. My concern is for my homeland and a population made diverse by post-war immigration. We are too small an island for multiculturalism. Our salvation is in exclusivity. The hijab is a statement of exclusivity. So are the round caps and the skullcaps and the Sikh turbans; and those indoctrinators of sacred apartheid, the religious schools: Catholic, Protestant, Jewish, Islamic. Or have we learned nothing from the travails of history? Has Ireland taught us nothing? The bloody horrors of India's partition? Is Scotland's chief minister, Alex Salmond, Scotland's Muhammad Ali Jinnah? Does he know or care what new antagonisms he fosters?

Who am I to ask? An overweight oldie footloose on a motorbike, so obviously irresponsible.

I haven't written of the slums, that vile Hogarthian world glimpsed down alleys. Nor did I photograph them. The denizens deserve more of us than to serve as illustrations for a travel book.

Indian Premier League 20/20 competition is in full swing. Sadly no matches at Kolkata's Eden Gardens before the first of April. Rajen and I make do with television. Sachin Tendulkar is God.

The colonel and I are invited to lunch by Kolkata's prophet of fusion cooking, Pradip Rozario. Pradip trained with the Oberoi Group both in India and in Europe. The Kurry Klub was his initial gamble. The first two years were tough. Next came KK's Fusion. And now Moi Amore on the top floor of a plush new shopping mall and cinema complex. The decor is light, smart and friendly. The food is delicious – giant tiger prawns lightly grilled. And we have a second invitation, this time to dine at Kolkata's Tollygunge Country Club.

Rajen warns that the dress code is smart casual. Our host's wife and teen daughter are definitely smart. So is Rajen. Our host is casual in a curly-collared short-sleeve sports shirt with a logo and boat shoes. I don't do casual. I have scruff or best. Best is bespoke trousers tailored in dark blue cotton at an attic sweat shop in Cochin's Jew Town. My navy shirt is hand-woven cotton (support the artisan) from the Rajasthan State Khadi Emporium in Jaisalmer. Add polished black brogues and a touch of hair gel and I look the works.

I am familiar with the historically notorious signs outside the clubs of Empire: No dogs. No Indians.

I am ignorant of today's restrictions: No Indian shirts.

With shirt collars obligatory, we are banned from the bars and dining room. Thus I am responsible for our party being consigned to eat in company with the mosquitoes in an open-sided marquee. I am desperately embarrassed by my faux pas. Rajen is naughtily delighted by the irony.

My last day in Kolkata and Rajen Bali promises me a treat. Off we march for breakfast, the colonel leading, three swings of his arms, three claps. Come on, chaps. First the South India Restaurant for breakfast dosa, then to buy prawns for my farewell supper.

Crows and a few dogs pick at a heap of stinking refuse outside the market. Why isn't it cleared away? Ask the municipal government.

The colonel has shopped at this market for 20 years. He selects limes, a red onion, barks witticisms at the stall holders, pokes at strange (to me) vegetables and fruit, explains their culinary usage – such is shopping with a two-legged encyclopaedia of the subcontinent's food.

A small skinny fish merchant scoops prawns from a basket for the colonel's inspection. The colonel approves. Fish gleam on a slab, no ice. Trussed chickens lie silent. Two black goats await the knife. A fresh carcass hanging from an iron hook drips blood into an open drain; a teenage butcher drags the skin from a second.

Guilt combined with embarrassment would have made me take a motor tuktuk back to the colonel's apartment. Rajen prefers a barefoot rickshaw wallah. Ever practical in his charitable endeavours, he has pushed up the rickshaw wallahs' wages by hiring them and always paying 15 per cent above the standard fare. Do this frequently and the raise becomes the norm forced on others.

Urged by the colonel, I am transporting the bike 560 kilometres north to Siliguri on the overnight sleeper train: 800 rupees for a second-class, air-conditioned sleeper, 800 rupees for the bike. Siliguri is the rail terminus both for Sikkim, the North East states and for the Toy Train to Darjeeling.

The Kolkata edition of the *Telegraph* ran a flattering piece on me this morning. I am stopped twice by bikers on the road to the station. Loading the bike is easy. First a porter empties the gas tank, then wraps the bike in straw and sacking, and wheels it down the platform. I watch as it is lifted into the goods van. The porter directs me to my carriage.

I occupy a lower level bunk across from an English woman. A child psychologist, she has been a Labour supporter since childhood and is a Labour councillor. The present Labour hierarchy disgusts her. She will either vote Liberal Democrat or abstain.

She is on holiday with a group off to trek in the foothills of the Himalayas. The word *trek* is Afrikaans, language of South Africa's white supremacists. Is *walk* inadequate? Less sexy? Less commercial? Presumably less socialist…

The lady asks what I have been doing in Kolkata.

Watch cricket on TV, drink beer and over-eat is a quick precis. Truth must sound boring to an outsider: that Rajen Bali and I talked – two septuagenarian chums sharing experiences and opinions and teasing each other. The teasing grows from affection and trust in a relationship. Rajen is a fine man, honourable, generous, determined in his principles, highly literate, widely read, widely travelled – and skilful in the kitchen. All in all, I am very fortunate old man…

Unloading the bike at Siliguri is a doddle. An employee of the Cindrella Hotel has brought a bottle of petrol. I lunch with the hotel's owner, Rajendra Baid. Politically liberal, he founded, at the age of 20, Siliguri's only newspaper. His purpose was to disseminate accurate and non-partisan information. The paper continues in profit despite electronic competition.

Lonely Planet describes the Cindrella Hotel as Siliguri's finest, bedrooms with polished floorboards. Finest, yes, but the floors are marble. Siliguri is cleaner than cities further south. The people seem different. I'm unsure in what way. Give me a few days…

I am remiss (stupid) in not having armed myself with a GoPro camera to mount on my helmet or on the bike. In Siliguri, I sit on a bar stool on the sidewalk for three hours at a back-alley tailor. The tailor is designing and sewing a headband that will hold my camera. The purpose? To shoot video as I ride.

The shop is ten feet by eight, two sewing machines, two tailors.

The younger, in his twenties, works on the camera headband. The older gives advice. The one-man chai shop opposite provides tea and further counsel. An elderly English speaker with a puncture repair shop (only for bicycles) translates. Add two or three onlookers and you have a street party. The street is clean. The people speak quietly, they don't jostle, they respect personal space. The only argument is financial. The tailor charges 50 rupees. I tell him, *Nonsense*, and pay double.

My camera lens is dirty. I buy a cleaning kit at a camera shop, unpack the kit in my hotel bedroom and squeeze a drop of cleaning liquid on to the lens. The spout shoots off the bottle. The entire contents flood the camera. Not only the lens but also the interior. Liquid bubbles float on the inside of the screen. Turn the camera on and the sole response from the computer is a request for the date. Were this the US I would hire a smart lawyer and sue the product manufacturer of the cleaning liquid for a new camera plus an extra million for mental anguish – settle for 100 grand. This is India. I weep.

Oh God, why hast thou forsaken me? Last night the camera disaster. This morning the laptop won't charge. An underweight young man sits on a plastic chair in a side-street shop that advertises laptop accessories. The shop is the size of a small shoe box. No accessories. Does he know of a computer mechanic? Yes, indeed. He pulls down the steel shutter on his empty shop and mounts an ancient kick-start mini Hero. I ride pillion. A right, a left, another right, a further left, each street marginally narrower than the last. All are clean. What joy after the garbage-littered streets of the south.

We park in the courtyard of a three-story concrete building, the builders of which had never met an architect. A side door opens to a tennis court-sized workshop, low-ceilinged, lots of pillars, no windows. Only one corner is occupied. Two apparently indolent male thirty-somethings are drinking tea. One of them has tilted a spotlight to illuminate a newspaper. I suspect that the bits of computer and computer shells have found a permanent home on two work-benches at right angles to each other. At such moments I remember the mantra with which my companion of Hispanic American travels, Ming, met all dangers and difficulties: 'Simon, we set out to have an adventure...'

I lay the laptop and charger on the workbench. The non-newspaper reader regards it with deep suspicion. 'It won't charge,' I say.

He pokes the charger with one finger. Nothing happens. I say, 'It's not a bomb.'

Relieved, he opens the laptop. I tell him that it has a Linux operating system. Possibly he understands.

He plugs the charger into a wall socket. The charger falls out. He strips the ends from two lengths of copper wire, wraps the prongs of the charger with wires, no insulation tape, and prods the enlarged prongs into the socket with a couple of skinny ballpoints. Inserting a diagnostic probe into the cable end that connects to the computer produces zero. 'It isn't charging.'

'Right,' I say.

'Do you wish me to mend it?'

'You can?'

'It is possible,' he says.

If only he sounded more confident.

Prying at the charger with a jeweller's screwdriver achieves nothing. A short discussion with my guide and the newspaper reader ensues before he takes a rusty kitchen knife from a drawer.

To me, 'You wish me to open it?'

'You're the surgeon.'

Fifteen minutes with a soldering iron and the charger works. 300 rupees. Old man of little faith...

Help Tourism develops tourism within the community. You will find them on the internet. Please support! Help Tourism's Siliguri office manager comes to the Cindrella Hotel in a four-wheel-drive Mahindra pick-up at 9 a.m. He has been instructed to transport me and the bike in the truck to a mountain camp on the side of the Neora Valley. I prefer to ride.

'The road to the camp is not possible.'

'So I will ride while the road is possible.'

Two roads lead from Siliguri to Darjeeling. The direct route passes through Kurseong. We take the westerly road that climbs close to the Nepalese border. The beginnings are a gentle climb through almost-flat tea gardens. Women pickers wade waist-deep amongst the apple-green bushes. Shade trees guard the lanes to tea factories and managers' bungalows. We cross and re-cross the narrow gauge railway that takes Darjeeling's Toy Train north from Siliguri. Then up and up and up...

Gone is the harsh heat of India's plains. Wisps of thin cloud or mist drift across the narrow road. Time to pull on waterproof over-trousers and a light windcheater. We stop at a tin-and-brick shack where a woman serves us sweet milk tea and momos (stuffed crescent-shaped dumplings) steamed by her mother over a wood fire. The women are of a different culture to those of the south. No humility here; these women own themselves. Their freedom is apparent in every movement and in the openness of their smiles and chatter.

I urge the driver of our pick-up to eat more. He is thin, young, married a year, first child born. His wife teaches in a private primary school – monthly salary 1,500 rupees. The driver earns 3,000 rupees plus 100 daily for food when away from home. A monthly family income of 40 pounds sterling – little wonder that he is underweight.

A grossly fat couple enter the chai shop. He is a doctor from Siliguri and boastful that his weekly visits to these uplands are an act of charity. His wife waddles behind the counter and helps herself to a packet of biscuits. The chai-shop daughter serves them bowls of vegetables and dal, plates heaped high with rice. The fat couple stuff their faces and leave without paying. As for us, down and down and down to a river gorge and a narrow village where tour agencies advertise white-water rafting. We cross a bridge and backtrack along the river. White water foams through the gorge. Two inflatable boats rest on a gravel spit. Tourists exchange tales of valour. How do I know? Been there, done that – though in Ecuador.

The road turns uphill – or up-mountain – once more into tea gardens. The ascent is steeper than any I encountered in the Americas. At one point the road tunnels under itself in a 360-degree turn. I was sweating in my windproofs down by the river. The sweat is chill now and I must fight a stiff breeze on my shoulder or be thrust towards the road's outer edge. How steep is the drop? How far is the drop? Don't know. Don't dare look. And what of the pain on my left side high under the ribs? Heart, muscular or too vivid an imagination? Scared? Yes. Suffering a couple of heart attacks does that to you. Calmness is essential. I breathe slowly and draw comfort from memories of the first pass I crossed in Mexico, a climb from 60 metres above sea level to 3,200. The pain was the same as were the fears – though with one added. Would the Brazilian-built Honda 125 fail? I rode 66,000 kilometres through the Americas. I have ridden 12,500 kilometres through India. Believe me, Honda 125s never fail… Not so the Mahindra pick-up.

The underfed driver parks the pick-up at a roadside shrine – not to pray but to lift the hood on a mini geyser. Brave, I peek down the mountainside. Four women pick tea on the near precipice. Do they never suffer from vertigo? At least they are sheltered from the wind that whips over the crest. Wind in mountains is always scary. The driver removes the radiator cap and rests the engine five minutes before adding water. I drag a thick jumper from my backpack. Onward and upward…

And upward…

The small mountain town of Lava is dominated by a modern monastery. The track to Help Tourism's camp is to the left on the final bend before the village. The manager assures me that the track is very bad, better take the bike in the pick-up. As if I can't cope… I'll show him. The track runs along the side of the mountain through a magnificent pine forest. The first few hundred metres are compressed dirt. Easy. Turn a bend and I face a climb over large smooth stones, first gear, bumpity bump bump bump. The stones kick the front wheel. Stay loose is the secret. Let the bike pick its own way as you would with a horse. A smooth stretch follows then more stones and a steep descent. Imagine a mountain stream without water. Downhill is always worse. Put both feet down, you lose the rear brake and begin to slide. Grab the front brake and you're on your butt. So, however scared, you have to keep going – which isn't easy when faced with a right-angle bend. The camp is 12 kilometres down the track. Twelve kilometres and 90 minutes – enough time to get accustomed to the conditions and gain faith in your ability and the bike's ability. Fun?

Yes, in bits and pieces. Forget the road as dry boulder-strewn riverbed. The straight stretches give magical glimpses of the valley between giant conifers. Ferns cascade from the uphill side of the track; rocks cocooned in moss, mirror-clear rivulets. Palest of pale-yellow butterflies chase each other, scent of leaf mould and pine tar – 12 kilometres of walker's bliss! Even the bad bits can't be that bad if a septuagenarian can handle them on a 125 commuter bike.

The turn to the camp is on the right under one of those square archways common to the subcontinent's Buddhist architecture. The final ascent to the parking lot is near vertical mud. I don't do mud. Nor does the Honda. We get three quarters of the way up before beginning to slip backwards. Add two-villager power and we make it. A wizened elf shod in gold rubber boots grabs my bags from the pick-up.

What is a camp?

What will I find? Presumably one or other end of cold-water basic…

Help Tourism's local director/partner, Uttam Paul, greets me with a silk saffron scarf and glass of locally brewed liquor that tastes of blackberries and is probably lethal. A flagstone footpath and stone steps lead to the comfortable porch of a one-bedroom log cabin. Within lies total luxury: polished wood floors, double bed with top sheet folded over blankets and duvet, near perfect mattress, small dressing room, bathroom with steam-hot water, thick towels. My only comment: Wow!

I write this on a bench on the log cabin's porch. The driver squats on the outer edge of the car park parapet (dead drop for ever), mobile phone to his ear – calling his wife, of course. How is the baby?

Villages the far side of the steep valley are a thin scattering of tin roofs on terraced patches of darker green amidst broad-leaf trees. Look beyond to snowcaps tinted with gold by the evening sun. There lie the Nathu La and Jelep La passes into Nepal and Tibet.

Stone steps bordered by ferns and bamboo lead to the dining hall on a higher terrace. Orchids droop between the rocks of the retaining walls. Three further cabins are occupied by holidaying families from Kolkata. The cabins have mezzanines and sleep four. Uttam Paul designed the buildings and oversaw construction by local villagers. His father was a doctor on a nearby tea estate. Uttam married locally and has a house in Lava. He is a neat, trim man in his early fifties who speaks quietly and strikes me as both gentle and thoughtful – qualities sadly mistaken for weakness in our modern culture. Uttam is tough-minded and a stubborn and dedicated fighter and worker for his community and ecology.

The three couples from Kolkata represent a pleasant facet of India's economic success – anti-TV, anti-computer games, pro-wildlife, pro-ecology. Sad that this attitude isn't more prevalent. Mid-age with young children, they explore, on holiday, the less known and less developed areas of India – mountains, nature reserves, wildlife sanctuaries, temples and fortresses less visited and difficult to reach. Their advice is to explore the north-eastern states. When I write of their advice I write of the three men. The women remain separate, care for the kids, talk amongst themselves, return to their cabins. A subservient species? What do I know? I am merely an observer.

Pale daylight seeps round the curtains as I pad to the bathroom for the fourth time in the night. Fresh out of bed my balance is never good. My spine and ankle and the knuckle on my right index finger hurt. Back to bed and I cuddle under the duvets – a few minutes to

5 a.m. and not much hope of getting back to sleep. I face a long ride through the mountains to Darjeeling and wish that I wasn't so tired. This journey has been too much for me. Just this once I'm writing the truth: that I'm scared of failure and scared of suffering some sort of physical collapse. I am 77 years old and having to get up in the night is standard. So are the painful joints. They don't matter. The heart scares me. I intend to keep going of course. I'll enjoy the journey most of the time. It is a great experience. But the fear is there and this wretched exhaustion. Enough of this melodramatic self-indulgence. I'll be scaring my children – that's if they read this account of my travels. Open the curtains and watch the dawn mist smoke through the trees; hot shower, drag on a thick jumper and sit out on the porch. The Neora Valley is a wildlife sanctuary and birds are abundant, though I can't name any. Ignorant old man...

Goodbye to Uttam Paul and the wizened elf in golden rubber boots. Rain fell in the night. The track will be slippery. Having ridden it once, I have nothing to prove. Sensible to load the bike into the pick-up.

Comfort is nil: bounce, bounce, bounce.

Walking would be pure pleasure.

We meet an Indian biker/film-maker at the track's junction with the road. He films us unloading the bike and I talk to camera – the usual stuff. Why I ride a small Honda: reliability, fuel consumption, light-weight manoeuvrability. And that there is nothing remarkable in what I do. Millions of people ride a bike to work each morning. All I do is ride further and enjoy a much better lunch.

Enough talk, get in the saddle: *Brmmm, brmmm...*

The road from Lava to Darjeeling winds all the way down through broad-leaf forest and all the way up to clipped tea gardens part hidden in layers of mist or low-lying cloud, hairpin turn after hairpin turn, harsh chill down to soggy sweat and back to chill. In Europe the road would be considered single track. Here pick-ups and eight-seaters squeeze by each other. No buses. Meet a truck and one or other driver pulls to the narrow verge. The drop is only a few hundred feet and is seldom sheer. Imagine rolling down through Kelly-green tea bushes. Not fun but interesting, and probably not fatal. Tin-roof cottages are little bigger than a council-flat living room back home. Village shops are smaller. Shiny packets of crisps hang above a tiny counter, open sacks of rice and millet, cigarettes, biscuits, a few bottles of soft drinks. The wind is less than yesterday. The nagging pain in my chest is the same as are the women carrying huge baskets supported on a headband. They respond to my *Hi* or *Namaste* with such open smiles, so un-Indian. Old men in wool hats salute with raised hands and flash pink gums. Old? I am probably older. It promises to be a good day...

The mountain town of Ghoom is an unplanned slum of concrete ugliness and garbage. A spur of Darjeeling's Toy Train runs down the main street. I took a fall in Colón, Panama, trying to cross the railway track at too acute an angle. Rails trapped the front wheel. Lesson learnt, I meet the track now at near 90 degrees.

Darjeeling sprawls along an even more precipitous ridge. The ridge was suitable as a site for a few boarding schools, small health spas, and summer bungalows for the British Raj. The modern town is a disaster. Small concrete hotels of unremitting ugliness crowd one another and squeeze into non-existence those few remnants of reasonable taste. A good shake would drop the whole mess down the mountain. Where is the planning authority, the urban administration? Are the administrators ashamed of their creation? Or are they blind to the awfulness? Perhaps they live elsewhere.

A Swiss baker built the Hotel Swiss in the 1920s as a family home and place of work. Now Help Tourism have the lease and run the hotel as a training ground for local employees. I follow the pick-up down a steep narrow road. The turn to the hotel is on a sharp corner and at an angle of 300 degrees. The gradient is even more acute. Three eight-seater Mahindras parked on the corner block the pick-up from making the turn. The driver waves me on. I creep in first gear. An Indian tourist seated in one of the Mahindras opens the door in my face. I can't hold the bike upright against the slope. Down I go, head in the ditch. A couple of drivers drag me and the bike upright. The Indian tourist continues chatting on his mobile.

Bollywood is shooting a movie at the Hotel Swiss. A tall, slim, very gay thirties wears a woolly hat with a bobble. I'm unsure as to his title but he's the man who makes things happen. He has no cure for a camera drowned in cleaning fluid. I traipse from camera shop to camera shop. Darjeeling scores an A-plus for vertical streets, an X-minus for camera technicians. The film crew eat packed lunches and packed dinners, leaving me as the only guest in the dining room. My head hurts. My shoulder hurts. My back hurts. My right knee hurts. These pains are to be expected in an old fool who falls off a bike (even riding at zero speed). Medication won't suffice. I need laughter and a smidgen of five-star luxury. The Swiss is a small charming heritage building and I am not registering a complaint. However, dispelling my misery requires more. For instance a bubble bath...

I have transported my miseries to what was the summer residence of the Maharajahs of Nazargunj and is now the Mayfair Hotel. The Mayfair does luxury. The manager throws wide the curtains on a close-up of cloud. No cloud and the view would stretch for a few hundred miles. When did the cloud last lift? February? Or was it January? Or December? I don't give a damn. Keep the view. Get rid of the manager (politely). Gush steaming water into the bath. Add a full bottle of Molton Brown hoarded from the Umaid Bhawan Palace. Hang the 'Do Not Disturb' sign on the door. Shush now. Don't even breathe. Grandpa is meditating in bubbly bliss...

I don't care for gloom – even historic, as in castles and Tudor manor houses. The Mayfair Hotel, Darjeeling, is a rare beast amongst heritage buildings: rooms are light. It is also a hotel where guests talk to each other. The library boasts six-seater sofas and opulently comfortable armchairs. Young barefoot diplomats on holiday from the

US Embassy in Kathmandu share a beer with a couple of Brits. All four were up before dawn to witness sunrise from the peak of Tiger Hill – in company with a few hundred Indian tourists. What did they see? Cloud. How was the cloud? Damp and depressing. Ah, well…

10

SIKKIM AND THE NORTH EAST STATES

Sikkim squeezes north between Nepal and Bhutan to poke Tibet in the butt. It was an independent kingdom until annexed by India in 1975. Gangtok is the capital, from Darjeeling some 100 kilometres. A good road from the frontier winds north through broad-leaf forest. All imports into and exports from Sikkim travel by this road. Beware trucks overtaking trucks on blind corners. And beware cars overtaking trucks that are overtaking trucks – also on blind corners. And beware local bikers speeding through minimal gaps. A thin drizzle and the tar is slippery...

The Mayfair resort is a couple of miles short of the city boundary. The resort is new, big and would benefit from a bulldozer – or a landslide. I have a reservation for one night. One night in company with a hundred or more middle-rank bureaucrats on a taxpayer-funded freebie is enough. And why would anyone else stay here? Room rates are too high for standard tourists; the rich would stay elsewhere. The resort doesn't make commercial sense.

What a great day! Firstly I have found a perfect place to stay and perfect company. Gangtok is on a mountain slope and spreads up and downhill from a long main street of mostly vile jerry-built hotels. Up slope is upmarket wooded gardens, the governor's residence, government offices, what was the king's palace before the Indians deposed the king, a Buddhist monastery. The Hidden Forest Retreat is down slope. It is small and is not built of concrete blocks. Quaint seems an adequate adjective. The owners are Sikkimese botanists in the Forest Department and the gardens are a delight of narrow paths dividing beds of joyous colour and leading to long glasshouses filled with orchids. Add good food, good conversation, a comfortable mattress and hot water – what more could an elderly traveller desire?

A small creeper-covered terrace with wickerwork easy chairs is a splendid place for afternoon tea with two charming and beautiful young women on holiday from Bangalore. Bangalore is India's IT capital. One of the women is a born-again Christian and has exchanged an excellent job for missionary work. I am instantly in love with the Himalayan-featured second woman who is not a born-again Christian. We sit together, sip tea, look across the valley to mountains hidden in cloud. And we talk…

Perhaps, more accurately, I get her to talk.

She is in her late twenties, unmarried, and lives with her parents who are Assamese (hence the Himalayan features). They moved to Bangalore in the pre IT years; property prices were reasonable, schools and university excellent.

My companion studied computer science. She is an executive in a US company that designs software. She visits the parent company in the US two or three times a year. She owns outright that ultimate status symbol of India's new middle class, a Suzuki Swift.

She has been going out two or three times a month for a movie or a meal with a young executive in another IT company. Under parental pressure she asked the young man whether they had a future – this shortly before coming on holiday.

The young man was horrified at the suggestion. He could never marry a Tribal…

This is a charming, warm, highly intelligent and beautiful woman. Were I of the right age and single, I would kneel at her feet, kiss her toes and beg for her hand.

She tells me not to be silly.

Silliness is obligatory in septuagenarians.

Perfect accommodation and now I have found a friend. Drive almost to the end of the main street before taking a left downhill. The

Rachna Bookshop is up a short ramp on your right. A notice on the window advertises poetry readings and film shows. Tall bookshelves are the background to comfortable chairs and a coffee table spread with magazines and newspapers. Atmosphere more private library than commerce makes the bookshop a natural centre for Sikkim's younger intellectuals. The owner's father was Sikkim's chief secretary in the years after the annexation and the owner lives with his parents above the shop. He is a natural organiser. He and friends are soon planning a visit north to Lachen and the rhododendron forests. I will need a Protected Area Permit from the State Home Department in addition to the Inner Line Permit. This could take a few days and offices are closed tomorrow for the weekend. A weekend of nothing would be wasteful…

Pelling is 110 kilometres west of Gangtok. Attractions are two monasteries, the holy Khecheopalri Lake and views of the world's third highest mountain, Kanchenjunga, if it isn't lost in cloud. The turn west off the trunk road south to the Indian frontier is at Singtam. The first section west from Singtam is up and down out of steep river valleys, hydroelectric dams under construction, brigades of bulldozers chewing the terrain, massive trucks tilling the road surface. Not pretty…

Then comes a biker heaven of good, narrow tar twisting and twisting up through pine forest and across apple-green slopes of tea, tea pickers bright spots of scarlet and purple, more forest, more tea, more forest, the joy of cool unpolluted air softly scented with pine tar. Pabong, Legship, Geyzing are the villages. Hurrying would be criminal; four hours in the saddle and I am only halfway.

A small, one-room tea shop four steps up from the road in the middle of nowhere boasts benches and two small tables. The proprietors are Sikkimese, the husband tall and muscular, wife petite. They eye me with suspicion. What possible reason would cause a foreigner to stop? And why is an old foreigner riding a motorcycle? The door opens on a short man, less Sikkimese in features. I sit at one table, he sits at the other. The husband serves him a large bottle of beer without being asked. I ask for tea – and is there soup?

The small man says, 'There is chicken soup.'

Chicken soup would be good.

The standard interrogation begins: nationality, job, marital status, children, grandchildren, and what do I think of Sikkim.

Sikkim is beautiful, particularly up here in the mountains.

'No dirty black Indians,' agrees the small man. He is the village schoolteacher. Ah, well...

The chicken soup comes with noodles. I slurp happily and head back outside for a further three hours of biker delight.

Pelling is a mountainside strip of small *Lonely Planet* land hotels. These hotels along the road are mostly owned by Sikkimese. A few bigger and newer hotels are downhill – Indian finance and Indian tourist territory. At an altitude of 6,000 feet, Pelling is cold once the sun sets. I arrive in thin mist and choose the first and oldest hotel on the strip. A wood fire burns in the sitting area. Eight hours in the saddle have earned me a good night's sleep. A quick shower, eat, take my pills and into bed, two thick blankets and a double duvet. Ah...

My new friends in Gangtok want to leave for the north on Thursday – one day here in Pelling before scurrying back to apply for the Protected Area Permit. I awake early to the first clear sky since arriving in Sikkim. A big terrace opens off the hotel sitting area. Gasping is in order followed by stunned silence. Imagine for a moment the background sky blue as blue. Paint across it an immense and fiercely jagged crystal line mounting to a central peak. The whole glows the softest of gold in the morning sunlight. Such is Kanchenjunga in all its snowy glory. Yes, silence...

The ride down from Pelling to Khecheopalri Lake is 30 kilometres of further joy. The narrow road is mostly tar and cut into a steep hillside. Ferns and bamboo flourish between broad-leaf trees; plunging rivulets of spring water spill long tails of spray between moss-coated rocks and boulders where minute wild flowers shelter; a light breeze draws soft shivers of brilliant harlequin-green along terraces of rice rising up the far slope. Cross the crest and the road dips again, shirt-sleeve temperature.

Khecheopalri village is a few cottages round a parking lot and a large notice enjoining silence and listing the forbidden sins of unseemly dress and behaviour, garbage-strewing, smoking, urinating.

The small lake shelters in a wooded cup, the surface still and clear. A footpath leads down through the woods. The faithful have built tiny prayer towers of small stones balanced one on another along the path; the sacrilegious have left candy and snack wrappers. The path ends in a small clearing at the head of the lake and a further notice:

> THIS PLACE OF WORSHIP IS PROTECTED UNDER GOVT.
> OF SIKKIM NOTIFICATION NO 701/HOME/2001 DATED
> 20.9.2001 THE PROVISION OF THE PLACE OF WORSHIP
> (SPECIAL PROVISION) ACT, 1991 GOVT. OF INDIA.
> DEVOTEES/VISITORS ARE THEREFORE APPEALED TO
> MAINTAIN THE SANCTITY OF THIS HOLY LAKE

A wooden jetty juts out into the placid waters; a wooden bench has seen better days. Two small men squat silent, perhaps in prayer. Bhutia is the name of the local people, categorised as Tribal – as was the young Assamese IT executive at the Hidden Forest Retreat; Tribal denoting primitive, inferior. Why must I give way to anger on such a glorious day? Breathe slowly, old man. Close your eyes. Meditate on the oneness...

Silence is ruptured by a coachload of Indian tourists calling back and forth as they descend the path. I watch as they crowd each other on to the jetty. One, a teenager, slaps a small bronze prayer bell suspended above a notice reminding visitors to shed their footwear on the jetty.

The two small local men watch in silence.

I give up on meditation.

First I take off my shoes; then, with many an apology, ease my way to the head of the jetty where I kneel in ostentatious prayer. And, kneeling, look up from the holy water and murmur to an elderly Indian tourist neatly dressed in Indian Gap, in appearance a pleasant man, 'It is polite not to wear shoes.'

Surprise is his first reaction, then a quick nod and just the one word, 'Correct.'

I return to my praying while he sheds his shoes and encourages his fellow tourists to follow suit.

Satisfied, I retrace my way to the bench in the clearing. I should feel some satisfaction at a small victory for righteousness. Mostly I feel shame.

I have been invited to base myself while in Sikkim at a recently opened Gangtok hotel, the Denzong Regency. The hotel is built in the upper section of the owner's family compound at the wealthier end of town. The picture windows of my room give on to a small balcony overlooking a lawn and pool; let the sky clear and Kanchen-junga's distant peaks are visible; so it will be from the hotel dining room where I study the menu three meals a day.

'The chefs need practice. Eat, eat,' encourages the hotel's owner.

Ah, such luxury!

And I have my Protected Area Permit. We leave for Lachen in the morning. Meanwhile my host wishes to have my heart checked by a cardiac specialist. At my age, and at this altitude and with my history, I must be at risk. Or so my host decides.

He is tall, grey-haired, and commanding. Of the Tibetan aristoc-racy, his family boasts two Dalai Lamas. His elder brother was the King of Sikkim's chief adviser. This is not a man to be gainsaid.

His chauffeur drops us at the clinic. My host leads the way across a crowded waiting room, knocks sharply on the door to the consult-ing room and, without waiting for a response, pushes me through.

The consultant is dressed in a plum-coloured velvet smoking jacket with matching bow tie. He sits in a wing-back armchair. Opposite him sits a patient in shirtsleeves. The patient takes one quick glance at my host, grabs his jacket and flees. I am ordered to sit. The consultant is commanded to take my blood pressure. Perfect...

My host demands a recheck. Normal...

My host humphs his disbelief.

The consultant scribbles an unnecessary prescription. We return to the car. The chauffeur drops us at the foot of Gangtok's pedestrian shopping street. I am marched to the pharmacy where my host delivers the prescription and departs on another task.

The pharmacist eyes me with some curiosity. 'You are staying with the Royal Gentleman?'

Royal, I don't know but regal? Yes, indeed...

The kindly owner of the Rachna bookshop has accompanied me to the Buddhist monastery above Gangtok. We are attending the equivalent of a Catholic sung Mass in the monastery's church. The abbot sits at the head of the nave, monks sit the length of the nave in three lines left and right, young boys in the front rows. We face up the nave to the abbot. Organ music and Gregorian chant accompanied High Mass at the monastic boarding school of my youth. Here the chant is accompanied by drums and bells. I don't mean to surrender to the drums and the chant. Surrendering myself is something that I haven't done in many years. I was with Vanessa the last time, before the sculpture of Lord Brahma the creator in the cave temple of Elephanta. Surrendering isn't something that you can do deliberately; taking a large dose of mescaline is deliberate but there is no certainty as to the character of the experience. Anyway that was all way back in the past. Back before Elephanta. Way, way back...

I feel myself going here in the temple and escape to sit on the parapet at the end of the monastery's flagged courtyard. Monks or visitors have been dropping garbage over the parapet. Smelling salts was the cure for faintness in the eighteenth century. The stink rising from the garbage is equally effective. The abbot should instruct the novices on ecology and issue them with garbage sacks.

We are a party of five. Travelling in a small Suzuki jeep are three Sikkimese in their early thirties plus a Goan chum from university days. I follow on the bike. We leave Gangtok early beneath its seemingly standard canopy of pale grey cloud. I have checked the map; the road is tar all the way; 120 kilometres is a doddle. First comes the steep winding descent from Gangtok, bends too tight for speed and I keep pace easily with the jeep. We are on the road an hour before pulling in at a roadside tea house. One of my companions, large in both height and girth, requires sustenance. Sun has broken through the clouds and we sit outside with views out across a wide valley, the far slope spotted with small steep fields and spruce.

Momos – dumplings – are standard fare in the Himalayas, in this case stuffed with minced lamb and served with a tomato and chilli dipping sauce of vicious heat. The tea house owners are escapees from Tibet. We are served by the daughter, a charmer on holiday from university where she studies economics.

China's ruthless occupation is a catalyst to talk of the Mayfair Resort where I stayed my first night in Sikkim. A casino is being added – no matter that gambling casinos are forbidden by both Buddhism and by Sikkim's laws. The bitterness is there in my companions, anger at the colonisation of their tiny country; anger at their parents for having resisted so feebly the annexation. The conversation is in English out of politeness to their guest yet I am not part of it – rather a stranger, who by accident, finds himself eavesdropping on private grief. The discomfort remains with me as I write. In 1937 an American's account of his life in a small Spanish town in the years preceding the Spanish Civil War was published. In his innocence, the American detailed the opinions of the townsfolk. Those of the left were arrested and shot. Am I, in writing now, mirroring the American's unwitting betrayals?

The road is a grey serpent squirming back and forth across a fierce snow-and-glacier-scoured terrain of mountain and river valley, dry wispy grass, small stands of spruce. The search is where and how to bridge the waters, always at the valley's narrowest point, the road hacked out of hill or mountainside. Beware of falling rocks. The sun gives our direction, north at first, then south for half an hour before turning west and finally gaining the Teesta River that leads north to the small town of Chungthang.

Confidence is always dangerous and I am confident. I am having a good day. The sun shines. I am in good company. This is a fun road for an elderly biker when taken slowly. We are on the eastern side of the river. Not yet in the monsoon and the riverbed is a wide spread of glacial boulders and small slow-running streams bordered by curls of gravelled beach. Mangan is the first village on our route that might be called a town. At 52 kilometres from Gangtok, we are almost halfway.

The valley narrows and the road zigzags steeply down to a bridge. Horror lies beyond the bridge. The road is being widened. Diggers and bulldozers have churned the surface into a mud and rock wallow. Kilometre follows kilometre of feet down and first gear. Simply keeping the bike upright is a struggle. The mountainside is almost sheer. One slip and down I go and heights scare me – or, rather, the fear of falling. Up ahead a worker waves a red flag.

My friends gather round while we wait, light cigarettes, ask if I am OK, suggest I ride in the Suzuki, one of them ride the bike. I long to agree. Pride stops me. Fear of being thought feeble, not a real man, a scaredy cat. The 'man thing' that women instantly recognise. Surely to God he can't be that stupid. Yes, he is…

Sirens herald the imminent explosion. Muffled thunder echoes across the valley followed by the rumble of falling rock. A bulldozer pushes the fresh fall off the road. So onward, scared, exhausted, stupidly stubborn, trying to prove a totally pointless point. Times such as this and I am so tired of myself, of being me, refusing to benefit from experience, endless repeats of the same mistakes. And wondering why I always associate dynamite with B-movie westerns.

Chungthang is at the confluence of the Teesta, Lachen and Lachung rivers. It is a small town enjoying a short-lived prosperity with hundreds of road workers eager to spend their wages. Trucks have spread mud in the street. Two minimalist restaurants are out of food. We sit at a table in the least depressing of the two, drink tea and munch soggy biscuits from an already opened packet. A crow would fly 50 kilometres to reach Gangtok. Distance by road is 82.

Roads in Sikkim's north are built to enable the Indian army to counter a Chinese land grab. Two roads fork north from Chung-thang. The right and major route leads to Lachung while we follow the Lachen River. The road is single-track tar, no roadworks and only two sections of zigzag. Lachen is at an altitude of 2,800 metres and the road climbs steadily beneath scurrying cloud. Sudden splashes of evening sun light the snow-tipped eastern peaks, while to the west all is gloom, dark spruce and scrub on the lower slopes, old snow clinging in high crevices.

Lachen is a tin-roof village of some 1,000 inhabitants thinly spread on the eastern slopes of the valley. They are a self-governing community with their own small parliament and their own rules and regulations. A monastery looks down on the village – or is sited nearer to God. The Mayfair Group have bought recently a modern barn of a hotel, more industrial architecture than good taste. Rooms are YMCA style, heating as a plus – this is a freebie so no complaints. Dinner is a thick meaty soup served in the dining hall. My compan-ions have beer on the table and are intent on making a night of it. I'm beat and head for bed.

We have been filming all morning in the Singba Rhododendron Sanctuary – or, more accurately, I was being filmed. Now we are picnicking beside the river. The filming didn't go well and a light but steady rain is a poor accompaniment for a picnic. One of my companions and I have been blowing on a spark beneath a handful of semi-dry moss and damp twigs. We do this squatting to keep our butts off the wet grass. I'm not good at squatting. My belly gets in the way and my thighs hurt; so does the ankle the Argentinian truck smashed in Chile.

Over to our left the bigger of our group, the one who eats the most, is watching a half-pack of beer cool in a pool. What fish there are in the river interests the Goan. A run of deeper water further down stream holds his attention. This is his first time in the mountains. Everything fascinates him. He is tall, thin, curly-haired, thick-rimmed spectacles, dark 24-hour beard. Cross a young culture hound let loose in the National Gallery with an avid and knowledgeable collector at a car boot sale and you have the picture.

The river is a good 150 metres wide here. It must be a fearsome sight in the monsoon, all foam and rocks and dead trees. For now it is shallow and split in five by banks of gravel. The mountain rises sheer at the far side. A few severely stunted silver fir or juniper have rooted in the deeper crevices, low tufts of coarse grass. Moss and the smallest of wild flowers must grow up there; they aren't visible in this light and at this distance.

Our chosen picnic spot, or what will be a picnic spot if we get the fire going, is on a flat strip perhaps a hundred metres wide that is probably awash when the river is in spate, though not flooded or the rhododendrons covering most of the strip would be dead. The few scrawny, half-dead silver firs sticking up from amidst the rhododendrons are leftovers from logging days. Logging is forbidden now and the silver firs are re-establishing their sovereignty over the flats and softer slopes.

A barrier across the road a kilometre further north is manned by wardens from the Forestry Department. The barrier marks the entrance to the Rhododendron Sanctuary. We are accustomed to think of a sanctuary as something small. At 45 square kilometres, Singba is more national park. A visitor centre a couple of kilometres beyond the barrier was opened this morning by the Minister of Tourism. The minister's arrival was presaged by a convoy of middle-rank officials on the make. The Mahindra four-wheel-drive six-seater is the vehicle of choice, diesel-engined polluters; the skin on an open carton of cream left in the fridge too long gives the colour. I was scheduled to be presented to the minister – an hour's wait for two

minutes of handshakes, a *How do you do* and *A pleasure to meet you.*
The one plus in the performance was an invitation to visit the minister in Gangtok.

Next came the filming. It started well, me on camera extolling
the beauties of the sanctuary, the extraordinary variety of rhododendrons. Unfortunately the rhododendrons are not yet in flower
and one bud looks much like another. Nor is rhododendron foliage
the most exciting of greens, particularly under cloud and in a light
drizzle. Colour is at ground level, moss on the rocks, tiny flowers
wherever you look, a myriad miniature rock gardens, utterly lovely.

I was in full flow, extolling these wonders of nature – this despite
rain dribbling inside my collar. Then I lost it. The garbage did for
me, either side of the road, a thin trail of soggy snack wrappers, cigarette packets, soft drink cans, plastic bottles. The necessary smile for
the camera slipped, the ersatz enthusiasm.

I was off script. What was I doing?

Surely it was obvious – picking up garbage. Someone has to…

And we have to get this fire going. Maggi noodles is the picnic
dish of the day; fire is a necessity.

One of our group drops a length of dead tree trunk by the fire as
a seat for the fire puffers. We have smoke – ironic as neither of us is
a smoker. And finally a very small flame…

Day two in Lachen and we have climbed 1,500 metres to the army
post on the mountain the west side of the valley. The road is a single-track zigzag of reasonable tar, first or second gear and no safety
rail. Thickish scrub and a few scrawny firs cling to the lower slopes.
The tar deteriorates on the approach to the army post and ends at a
lifting barrier guarded by two sentries. The road beyond the barrier
is rutted gravel both sides of a central ridge. The Honda isn't at its
best on wet stones and ruts. Nor am I. The barrier is a blessing…

A few prefabricated and immaculately painted huts squat on the
upper side of the road. Regimental and national flags fly above the
small office on the left where the sentries keep watch.

Indian soldiers are tall and smartly dressed. Enviable headgear for this regiment is a padded khaki cone wound at the base with a thick wide band of tartan cotton. The sentries are followed out of the office by a young lieutenant.

Our presence is explained: that our Goan friend has never experienced snow close enough to touch. The snow line is up a further few bends beyond the barrier. Please, can we pass…

I am the main concern – a foreigner in a military zone this close to the frontier. The lieutenant considers while inspecting my passport and my Inner Line Permit. I pray that the he will let the Suzuki through while holding me until their return. No such luck.

Six further bends to our goal, altitude is 4,500 metres, front wheel slithering, scary stuff. Our Goan friend stands in the snow to have his picture taken. I am photographed gazing out over the valley. Grey scudding cloud hides the peaks. In the photographs I look quite valiant.

Back to Gangtok tomorrow, the sybaritic luxury of the Denzong Residency and the Royal Gentleman. One of my companions will ride the bike over the bad stretch.

Gangtok is a pleasure. The Rachna bookshop is pure joy and the Royal Gentleman is an informed and interesting conversationalist. I head for Assam tomorrow where I am invited to stay with the Royal Gentleman's sister and her husband, younger brother of a Raja.

This morning I visit the Minister of Tourism.

Sidekicks or sycophants occupy two sofas off to the side in the minister's office. I shake hands with the minister and take a chair facing his desk.

The minister asks for my impressions of Sikkim.

Wonderful.

And the Singba Rododendron Sanctuary.

Equally beautiful – except for the garbage. I am well prepared and into my spiel before he can take umbrage. My proposal will make him famous. Six months and organisers of the planet's ecological conferences will be begging for his presence. I leave the lecture fees, limos, first-class air travel and five-star hotels to the minister's imagination.

Each passenger in a car visiting the sanctuary will be given a strong bag made from recycled paper at the barrier. Printed on the bags are two slogans.

On one side: NATURE IS GOD'S GIFT TO MAN.

On the reverse side: DISCARDING GARBAGE IS A SIN.

Sin is the operative word. Law is meaningless in India.

Visitors hand in the bag prior to leaving the sanctuary. The bag must be full. Failure to comply earns an immediate fine of 1,000 rupees.

What if they don't have any garbage? asks the minister.

I reply that there is enough along the side of the road for everyone. A year at most and the sanctuary will be pristine and the minister can downsize the bags.

'And you will be famous…'

The sidekicks and sycophants chuckle while the minister considers. His sudden anger is obvious – perhaps the chuckles were the spur.

'They are all the same,' he says, 'those filthy black Indians…'

Study a map for a moment and it becomes obvious that India is territorially nonsensical. The Siliguri Corridor that connects Sikkim to what I think of as mainland India is a mere 30 kilometres wide. Squeezed between Bangladesh and Bhutan, the corridor from mainland India to Assam and the North East States is little wider. Geographically, neither belong – not a statement to endear me to India.

I am to deliver gifts from the Royal Gentleman to his sister. He bids me farewell and off I wobble south again down Highway 31A. 31C is the road to Assam and the only road link between mainland India and the North East States. The intersection is 20 kilometres short of Siliguri. Nagrakata is the first town of any size.

Those expecting to speed down a six-lane highway will be disappointed. I don't speed. I prefer not to do trucks. 31C is trucks, trucks and more trucks...

In shape, Assam is a stump-legged body sprawled on its back. The great Brahmaputra River is the spine. Assam is wet, rainfall ranging from 1,800 mm in the east to upward of 3,000 mm in the west. Ten kilometres short of the state frontier and I am in a heavy drizzle. Trucks queue in three long lines at the frontier, wheels sunk inches deep in slushy mud. No evidence of movement.

A few police, state, national or whatever, lounge outside the Customs office. I find a tea house and a truck driver that speaks English of a sort. Once he was held up at the frontier for three days. Hispanic American frontiers are the same. Drivers are paid by the load. Three days is financial disaster. The poor always pay.

I sneak through between the trucks and am on my way.

No mountains for the first time in a month. Rice paddy spreads either side. The highway crosses the erstwhile princely state of Cooch Behar. The British ranked Maharajahs in importance. Top Maharajahs were granted an 18-gun salute, fewer guns for lesser Maharajahs. Orchha was 15, Cooch Behar 11. No guns for Rajas...

A right in Bongaigaon on to Route 318 leads to the bridge across the vast Brahmaputra River at Goalpara. The bridge carries the railway on the lower level, roadway above, a two-kilometre ride within a steel cage. Now only one more hour to ride, if I don't get lost...

My destination is a small town of minimal importance other than to those who live there. No ugly modern development disfigures the town. No tourists. Main Street is small houses, small shops. Late afternoon on a rainy Sunday and the shops are closed – this is a unique experience for me in India. A lone pedestrian is sheltering under an immense baobab tree outside a school. I have checked on Google Translate and memorised the Hindi. 'Raja ke ghara,' I ask with confidence. The Raja's compound...

The pedestrian looks blank.

Surely he understands Hindi. Perhaps he is deaf – or an imbecile. Or is this that common instance of *I'm a stranger here myself*?

Tired and frustrated, I head on up the road. Three men sheltering under two umbrellas stand talking on the pavement in front of a wall poster advertising Spoken English and Personality Development. The men can't all be visitors. Yet 'Raja ke ghara?' is met with a shared incomprehension.

A second attempt, annunciation slow and clear, is met with equal puzzlement.

Frustration transforms me into that horror of horrors, the British Blimp Abroad. Shout loudly in English and everyone understands. 'King House! King House!'

'Ah, King House,' they say and point back down the main street to a clipped grass sward the size of a couple of football pitches. 'King House…'

Dipping my head in shame is justified. Joining my hands together as in prayer is stupid. '*Namaste*,' I manage once before losing my balance. I have been in the saddle 10 hours. What strength my legs had is gone. Over I tip into the road – proof indeed that pride comes before a fall.

Further guilt as the men dirty their clothes in lifting me and the bike from the gutter. One steadies the bike while the other two make vain efforts at making me presentable.

'Please,' I beg, definitely English, but no longer a Blimp, 'Please, I'm so sorry, so sorry, such a nuisance…'

Big trees surround the grass sward. Three small family temples of faded ochre face across the sward to the high walls surrounding the Raja's compound. Heavy double doors with brass bolts and massive padlocks are the ceremonial entrance to the compound crested with sculpted full-size lion and unicorn standing upright on their hind legs, a trident between them. Word must have spread of my arrival. My hosts await me. They stand arm in arm beneath a porte cochère to the right of the main entrance. Both are dressed in loose summer whites, her trousers more voluminous than his. She wears a wide-brimmed straw hat; his is a somewhat battered panama. It is a very English scene; grass, trees, old walls, and this couple in their late-middle age are very English of their class. Their greeting of this wet dirty guest is equally English, as if I was a close cousin accustomed to coming down from London for the weekend.

A side door opens off the porte cochère. The Raja's Durbar Hall faces the main gates. In three sections, it is a rectangular building on two floors. Roofs are of corrugated tin painted a red faded by the sun and extending to shade the upper windows while half-glazed French windows on the ground floor open to a deep verandah. English settlers built similar houses in Africa and the Caribbean. Even the carved wooden trim to the roofs is familiar as are the flower beds sloping up to the verandah. The 'King House' is to the rear, similar architecture to the Durbar Hall, deep verandahs on two floors, the centre projecting between identical wings.

My hosts lead the way beneath an arch of climbing roses to a part-flagged patio with, on three sides, toy cottages matching in style: kitchen and dining room are in one, my hosts' bedroom and sitting room to the right, two guest bedrooms opposite.

'Tea, or would you prefer to change first,' asks my hostess. *It's just us,* would have been added in my youth so that I would know not to dress (dress being black tie and dinner jacket).

A gardener carries my bags. An elderly maidservant kneels and bows to touch her forehead to my filthy shoes. 'No,' I almost screech, 'please don't…'

A good night's sleep prepares me for adventures. First we visit a 'Tribal' market out in the country. Am I alone in finding Tribal a worrying term?

The market is ringed by trees and sheltered by plastic awnings. Stalls are mostly a few vegetables piled on a sheet of newspaper. No humble, self-effacing women here; these ladies compete in raucous humour with the rowdiest of Catalan market traders. Dress is mostly turquoise below the waist with yellow above, though only shoulders visible above a comforter of saffron cotton.

A young man sitting cross-legged oversees a double line of seed packets. Each packet is cut at one corner. Customers squat to watch as he shakes seeds carefully into his palm, counts the required quantity and screws them into a scrap of newspaper. Coins change hands.

Dried river fish in progression of size are piled along two folding tables set end on end, silver minnows, mini fillets dry as autumn leaves, large fish a deep mahogany.

A tall lady has been on the hooch. She has one tooth, a small clay pipe clenched between her gums. She removes the pipe to shout at my host that she wants to marry me. My host says that he fears a riot and off we drive to picnic at the family's rubber plantation.

Rubber trees are a reminder to me of Guatemala and the approach to what was my uncle's *finca* high on the Pacific side of the volcano that dominates Lake Atitlan, and of my friend Eugenio's *finca* that he has developed into a resort on the river below Fronteras. Column upon column of silver-grey tree trunks support a feathery canopy; milky-white sap oozes from a shallow gash in each trunk into tin cups.

I recall being told in Bombay (now Mumbai) by the mother of a university friend of Vanessa's that Mrs Gandhi never forgave a slight. She had been a student at the same private girls' school as Mrs Gandhi. Many students were Rajputs, their families large landowners. They believed themselves socially superior to Mrs Gandhi and treated her with some contempt. Mrs Gandhi's revenge was laws restricting land ownership to 50 acres. Large tea, sugar and rubber plantations were exempt – Mrs Gandhi was either indebted to the owners or nervous of their influence.

Small-town Rajas were of small account and 200 acres don't count as a large plantation. My host's family has been fighting in the courts for 20 years to retain ownership of their land.

The plantation's processing plant is an open-sided shed with six rows of wood pillars supporting a tin roof, concrete floor. Bare-leg workmen weigh buckets of sap before pouring it into shallow moulds where the sap coagulates. The coagulated rubber is fed through steel rollers to form sheets which are hung to cure in a smokehouse. The process is labour intensive. Labour in India is less costly than in Guatemala where the plantations sell the sap to centralised industrial processing plants.

We eat our picnic on the office terrace. An extended family of golden langur watch us from high in the tall trees. These monkeys are an endangered species native only to this region of Assam and to the Black Hills in Bhutan.

The scene seems idyllic, yet my host's elder brother was kidnapped on this plantation by Assamese nationalists. The family had to sell their last piece of urban property to pay the ransom.

My thoughts drift to Guatemala where the forest people were accustomed to harvesting sap from wild rubber trees. A 10-litre can of sap would keep a family in flour for a month. The Planters Association claimed that this trade encouraged the stealing of sap by their own labourers. A law now forbids processing plants from buying rubber from any but registered plantations. So it goes, so it goes…

We are sipping fresh lime and soda on the cottage verandah. My hostess sits in an upright chair, bare feet, one leg tucked under the opposing thigh. My host lies at ease beside her in a planter's chair. He is bald-pated with a fringe of white curls. Black streaked with grey, her hair in a thick glossy plait that falls loosely between her shoulders. In skin colour he is paler than me, features barely hinting at the Asiatic. His wife's Tibetan heritage is more pronounced and she is the taller by a centimetre or two and younger by at least 15 years.

They met while he was teaching at Gangtok's premier private high school – a decidedly lowly career. Youngest son of a small town Raja, he was Hindu and divorced. She was the Buddhist offspring of Tibetan aristocracy. Their elopement was a great scandal. Her eldest brother exiled her from the family compound. Only with his death has she been permitted to visit. The Royal Gentleman is now head of the family. He dotes on his sister and on her husband and is building them a cottage next to his own home below the Denzong Residency – a welcome retreat from the oppressive heat and humidity of the Assamese summer.

I am resting in the second planter's chair. We talk for a while of books. Vanessa reaches for my hand. It is so natural to love and be loved. Have I dozed for a moment? I leave in the morning...

Guwahati, capital of Assam, lies on the south bank of the Brahmaputra River. It is an easy ride on a good road across flat arable country. I am here to apologise to the central government's head of tourism. She had invited me to visit with her the Manas National Park that stretches for over a hundred kilometres along the Bhutan border and was once the hunting preserve of the Maharajahs of Cooch Behar. I preferred to visit the Royal Gentleman's sister and her husband. Now, filled with guilt, I assure her that I am a passionate advocate of Assam's fauna and that I am riding tomorrow directly from Guwahati to the Kaziranga National Park. I mention my excitement in having seen golden langur. Mollified, she decorates me with a folkloric straw hat and a floor-length scarf of white linen. We stand side by side to be photographed. She looks sophisticated. I look weird.

One night in a modern hotel with two elevators in the city centre has left me knowing nothing of Assam's capital city. Ahead is a ride east of only 200 kilometres to the Kaziranga National Park. The road clambers from Guwahati up over a steep spur before descending to the planes that slope down to the Brahmaputra River. Wooded hills rise gently to the south of the road. Tea grows on the lower slopes beneath trees sprinkled with silk-threaded puffs of white blossom and trees shade the road. Traffic is minimal. I am enjoying the ride.

Two female elephants and a half-grown calf amble along the other side of the road. The females carry branches of green leaves in their trunks much as women of my mother's generation carried handbags. I pass a chain of primary-school children, each with a satchel. The children wave. Yes, this is a very good day. And a thought strikes: I haven't been terrorised by a truck or bus driver since unloading the bike from the sleeper train at Siliguri. Near-death experiences were common in mainland India, one or two a day. Sikkim and the North East States are different.

A large road sign welcomes me to Kaziranga. I have checked online and know that the park is 430 square kilometres and home to two thirds of the world's one-horned rhinoceroses – or should that be rhinocerosi? Tall elephant grass stretches down to the forest edge. The Brahmaputra must lie beyond. Deer, probably samba, graze near the road and I spot elephants against the tree line. Far away in the distance mountains rise out of a thin duvet of white cloud or mist.

The official entry to the park is in a small shady village boasting a few minimalist stores and tea houses for the locals, a marginally smarter restaurant (vegetarian and non-vegetarian) and that necessity of modern living, an internet café.

As instructed, I pass through the village. The Wild Grass Hotel is a further couple of kilometres on the right side of the road. The owner is a relative or a university friend of someone I have met on my travels – I am not sure who.

He is a tall man, determinedly commanding. I am inspected.

'You look tired,' he says. 'You are a writer. Stay here and write…'

Servants are ordered to unload my luggage and lock the bike in the garage. I am led past a baronial dining hall that should have a minstrel's gallery at one end but doesn't. A wide, arched doorway opens off a windowed verandah to steps down to a tree-shaded lawn. Bedrooms are beyond in a lopsided modern building of four levels on one side and three on the other. I find a reminder of Tudor construction in the skeleton of heavy pillars connected by equally heavy beams, though of concrete rather than green oak. Walls painted terracotta are inset into the skeleton. Bedrooms open either side of a staircase that would suit a larger building. Each bedroom has windows to the front and to the side; each window is in three sections; each section has 10 panes – again strangely Tudor.

I am on the second floor. My room is big, so is the bathroom. Floors are polished wood, double bed, armchairs and a writing table in the window that overlooks the lawn. I unpack and return to thank my host only to be told that he has left for Guwahati.

He has given instructions that I am not to leave until his return.

When will that be?

The manager shrugs. Two or three days, possibly a week. Perhaps he will visit Delhi…

I am imprisoned – an enchanting prison. The sentence is indeterminate. Hard labour is tapping two-fingered on the small keyboard of my faithful Asus EC notebook for three or four hours of an afternoon. Will my host demand to inspect my output? Grade my work? If unsatisfied, pass a further sentence of delightful incarceration?

And I have a friend, a young lady from Surinam via the Netherlands from where she has recently gained a masters degree in criminology. Deidre's travels in India are a break from study, time to decide on her next move. I insist that a doctorate will open doors to fascinating careers. Deidre counters that she has spent the last six years doing nothing but study – six years is enough.

We meet for breakfast each morning in the baronial dining hall before being driven in one of the hotel's open Suzuki mini jeeps to the park. Company of a park ranger is obligatory. The ranger directs us to where he hopes we will see a tiger. See a tiger and he expects a massive tip. We are satisfied by what we do see: deer of various kinds, buffalo, elephants, a wild boar, jungle fowl and many a rhinoceros. Rhinoceros are comic when seen from behind. They are broad in the butt and the armour on their backside sags – a fat, short-legged elderly woman in baggy bloomers.

Odd how some hotels attract guests with common interests and offer a friendship to be cherished. The Bundelkhand Riverside in Orchha was one. Wild Grass is another.

Not all is happiness. Deidre has been pestered for the past two days by an Assamese professor of mathematics on holiday from his university. The professor drinks – not to extreme excess but sufficiently to make him verbose. He is accustomed to a captive audience and he has a tiresome habit of leaning across the table when he talks. Up close his breath smells.

Late afternoon and I have finished my hard labour. Deidre has been waiting for me at a table on the terrace. The professor has taken a seat opposite Deidre and is in full spate. My arrival irritates him. He ignores me.

'I was wondering, are you Tribal,' I ask.

My question snaps him upright. 'Certainly not.'

'Then what are you?' I ask.

He is stumped for a moment. Then, 'People,' he says. 'We are people.'

'So Tribals aren't people?'

'That's not what I said.'

'It is exactly what you said.'

Deidre smiles sweetly and suggests we take a stroll in the garden before dinner...

The owner of Wild Grass has returned. I am released from custody – released on licence. My instructions are to report to the owner's sister at the family compound in Guwahati. This sister is his youngest sibling, hence named Baby by her parents – a fun name when a child; somewhat inappropriate for an oversized and widowed schoolteacher in her fifties. The compound is in a low-rise district pre-dating the city's post-independence expansion. Take a left at the next intersection and you find traditional shops, a restaurant or two, a cobbler, silversmiths, laundry, even an upstairs cybercafé that doesn't serve coffee.

The owner of Wild Grass has an office on the right front of the family compound; his elder brother has a two-level house to the left; Baby's bungalow is at the rear, no street noise, peaceful. A married couple cook, clean and do the laundry. Their relationship to Baby is more friendship than servant. Baby tutors their daughter in company with other primary-school children after school.

I am offered tea on my arrival. We sit at the dining table. Children are taught at this table. Many a battle has been enjoined over lack of preparation or incomplete homework. Baby is loving, never a pushover, expert at eliciting the truth and accustomed to victory. I am under cross-examination. Where have I been, what are my plans?

To explore a little of the North East States...

'Wherever you are going, you will be coming back here,' Baby says. 'No need for you to be carrying everything...'

My bags are carried through to the spare bedroom. Baby shows me the light switches and how to operate the shower. Thus I have a home from home for the last weeks of this Indian odyssey. I also gain a social life thanks to Baby's home being the rendezvous for friends from town and out of town. Most, if not all, were beneficiaries of a Catholic education in Shillong where St Edmunds and Loreto Convent have served Assam's landed, commercial and professional classes from early in the twentieth century.

Baby teaches at the dining table. I fight India's internet. The problems are standard. Either the server is down or, when it works, a power cut hits midway through uploading. Sending pics to illustrate a travel piece on Sikkim takes two days of frustration. A piece I sent BA was lost in the ether. Add that cybercafé cubicles are cramped and sweaty and a hunting ground for mosquitoes. This is the downside. Delightful is Baby's company. She spoils me. The cricket 20/20 World Cup is on television in the late evening. Baby has a large-screen TV in her bedroom. I sit on an upright chair beside the bed.

'That chair is not comfortable,' Baby says. 'Better you sit on my bed.'

I remain on the chair.

'No need for fear,' says Baby. 'I am not attacking you.'

I ease one leg across. A half-hour passes before the second follows. Baby has been asleep an hour before I finally gain sufficient courage to shift my backside. England performs brilliantly. The game finishes. I sneak off to bed. One further embarrassment, the television controls were beyond the understanding of my Neanderthal mind.

'Why were you leaving on the TV?' Baby asks at breakfast.

The end of a journey should have a suitably valiant ending. I have decided to ride over the Sela Pass to Tawang in Arunachal Pradesh. The head of the pass is 4,000 metres above sea level. The total distance is 500 kilometres. None of Baby's friends have been to Tawang so road conditions are a mystery; Baby considers the journey unwise. It is also complicated by the requirement for a Protected Area Permit. This might be easier if my mobile's SIM card functioned in Assam. It doesn't and obtaining a SIM card that does function requires a further permission. Permission is difficult and anyway would take longer than I have.

I consult a travel agent with a reputation as a fixer. More complications: Protected Area Permits are not issued to solo travellers. A group of four is the minimum permitted entry. However (in India there is always a *however*), the fixer knows an Arunachal Pradesh politico with influence in the state capital, Itanagar. Allow three or four days…

'What was I telling you,' says Baby. 'So many problems…'

Four days is sure to be a week. Baby suggests I visit Shillong. 'Very beautiful,' she assures me. 'So green and always cool. Many visitors say that it is the same as being in Scotland.'

Favoured for its climate, the hill station of Shillong was capital of Assam under the British. The town and surrounding hills were hived off in 1972 to create Meghalaya, India's smallest state. Unusually for India, lineage and inheritance are matrilineal, though with a caveat that might disturb a feminist's first approval. All wealth is inherited by the youngest daughter. She, in turn, cares for the parents.

The only road connection to Meghalaya is from Guwahati. The rise in altitude from Guwahati is 1,500 metres over a distance of 90 kilometres. Surface is good, though with heavy truck traffic and the resulting diesel fumes. Broad-leaf woods give way to pines; cropped hill-slopes suggest overgrazing. Meghalaya has the highest rainfall of any state yet water looks critically low in an immense dam to the right of the road.

Central Shillong has hardly changed since the days of the British. Here is the sprawling military cantonment, government offices, houses of the senior administrators. 1920s Tudor Suburban is a favoured style.

Baby has a friend from school days with an interesting husband. I am to telephone once I arrive. Telephoning isn't easy without a SIM card. The solution is a café where I rent the waiter's SIM card for one call at exorbitant cost. Baby's friend is married to the president of the Vintage Car Club. He has created surely the only art deco mansion in the North East. Here is Miami at its best. Every detail is exact. For perfection an art director would add a couple of Cuban gays in shorter than short shorts cruising by on rollerblades.

The garage is equally surprising. Pride of place goes to a 1950s Studebaker parked beside a 1930s Morris 8 open tourer. A Second World War US Army jeep is equipped with the original jerrycan and trenching tool and a 1940s BSA 500 (bike, for the ignorant) is in mid rebuild. Members of the Shillong Royal Enfield Riders Club are coming to the house this evening.

We drive out today to a picnic spot in the hills above Shillong. We are Ashok, his wife Rula, and me in Ashok's classic jeep. A dozen members of Shillong's Royal Enfield Riders Club are the escort. A dozen Bullets produce an impressive rumble.

What do we do? What such people do in Iran or Texas or Argentina, Pakistan, France or Russia – or back home at the Horizons

Unlimited June meet. We drink cold beer and whisky (not mixed), eat what is easy to cook over an open fire, tell tall tales of rides done and planned, and sing to a guitar. The quality of the singing varies. Not much else! Thanks guys for a great day. And my thanks to Ashok and Rula for warm and wonderful hospitality in their lovely home. A good many years have passed since I last danced with a billiard cue to Frank Sinatra and the Andrews Sisters.

Baby welcomes me back with pork simmered with bamboo shoots and Naga chillies rated the hottest in the world. I admit to Baby at breakfast that I am a dosa addict. So is Baby. A restaurant on the next street serves great dosas – though not for breakfast. We will lunch there on my return from Arunachal. The permit for Arunachal was promised for Monday. I get it mid-afternoon Tuesday, too late to leave. The permit is for 21 days and lists where I may visit.

I am travelling light, one backpack. The rest stays under the bed. Having a base makes life so much easier. I am expected for the night at the Eco Camp in the Nameri National Park where another of Baby's many friends is the manager.

'Remember the turn at Balipara,' warns Baby for the umpteenth time.

The sensible route would be south of the Brahmaputra River and across the Kolia Bhomora Setu Bridge a few kilometres short of Kaziranga. I prefer new territory. The Saraighat Bridge outside Guwahati is another rail and road double-decker, though only 1.3 kilometres long. Roads beyond are raised against frequent flooding, crumbling stretches, slow going but worth the effort for the villages and trees in full flower – mimosa and the magnificent pride of India blanketed with pale lavender blossom.

To the small town of Balipara takes three hours. I mind Baby's repeated warnings and check with locals at the main intersection for the Nameri road. Locals have little interest in eco sanctuaries. They are familiar with the Nameri Tea Plantation. I find myself 35 kilometres off track. Dumb? Yes, of course.

Worse is to return to Balipara and stop at the crossroads to consult the road atlas. A young man accosts me. Am I going to the Eco Camp? The manager has sent him. He will report my stupidity. This, in turn, will reach Baby's ears. I imagine the conversation. 'How you can be so silly, Simon? And after I was warning you.'

Assam's Nameri National Park abuts the Pakke Tiger Reserve in Arunachal Pradesh, 1,000 square miles of forest. A dirt track leads through the trees to the Eco Camp. Originally founded by a fishing club, it lies adjacent to the banks of the Jia Bhareli River, habitat of India's premier game fish, the Himalayan golden mahi.

The camp is a circle of large tents under thatch. Each tent has a bathroom at the rear. The bathrooms are tiled, showers heated by butane geysers. The manager is Noel to his family and school friends, Ronnie to everyone else. He is tall, slim, grey-haired, was educated (along with most every other male I meet socially in the North East States) by Irish Christian Brothers at St Edmunds, Shillong, and speaks tea garden English. Tea garden English is English public school with a 1940s vocabulary and a slight Indian accent. The Club was the centre for tea garden society (tennis, billiards, dances, decorous flirtations). Terrorism did for the Club – Assamese nationalists building personal fortunes from kidnapping. Noel opted out. He remains out, though maintaining contacts worldwide.

He sits on a bamboo bench on the central lawn in company with a Sikh army officer dressed in shorts, sandals and a T-shirt. The Indian Army in the North East States is in two parts. The main army guards India's frontiers against possible Chinese incursions. Other units specialise in counter-insurgency. Of the latter, the good ones do much of the crime-fighting that the police can't or won't do. Illegal logging, brigandage and so on. This Sikh from the Punjab is one of the good ones. He is a big, burly bruiser of a man, soft spoken, newly married, angered by Civil Administration's incompetency in law enforcement.

Drinking chilled Foster's in Noel's one-bed thatch-roof bungalow is immensely pleasurable. Noel was one of a gang of bright kids from

St Edmunds who made it to Delhi, India's premier university. Now he reads omnivorously. A friend from Delhi days, a leading literary critic, passes on books sent to him for review. Books pack shelves, form piles on every table, overflow into unlikely corners. Add sculpture, paintings, even a David Bailey portrait of Noel's sister, and the sitting room should feel overcrowded. It doesn't. It feels comfortable. I am reminded of my early twenties in Kenya and visiting British district commissioners in the Northern Frontier District or the hills, men who are routinely mocked today as buffoons or twits but who ruled over vast areas not by force but through wisdom and a desire to benefit the people. They were cultured men with first class honours degrees from good universities in a day when a first was hard to come by and demanded original thought. Above all, they were incorruptible and believed a career of service was more rewarding than accruing wealth. So there I am, revealed in my true colours: an old-fashioned British Blimp. The colonel in Rajen Bali would be proud of me. So would Rajen, the writer...

A hornbill sounds reveille at the Eco Camp. Hornbills whistle sweetly. The whistle ends with a deep and very loud honk. Think rubber-valve water pump. A woodpecker is next to wake and goes on and on. The only Indian cuckoo is surprisingly gentle in his call. Perhaps he has a hangover. I feel fine.

Noel and I have been invited to early breakfast by the Sikh commander at the tented army camp. For Noel this is a first in the five years of his managing the camp. The commander has been operational all night and hasn't had time to change. Breakfast is an English fry-up of eggs and bacon. I depart with an invitation to dinner on my return and a warning that the road is bad.

Bad has many meanings from heavy traffic to potholes, sharp bends, uneven surface. The frontier is five kilometres. I present my passport, visa, vehicle documents, Protected Area Permit. Details are entered with utmost care in a massive ledger. An armed border guard lifts the barrier. I am in Arunachal Pradesh. Ahead tower the Himalayas.

The first few kilometres are bad as in a few potholes. No problem. This is an adventure. I feel good. Weep for the unwary…

The major is Special Forces. Special Forces jump off cliffs for fun. They wrestle tigers, skydive, speed-march deserts, ski black runs with full backpack and sub-machine gun. Special Forces bad is bad. I am in mud. Deep mud. Boulders camouflaged by mud. Two hours to cover the first 10 kilometres is good progress. My survival is luck and following locals on bikes – though two locals fall, mud head to foot.

This is not fun.

This is scary.

Riding from Gangtok to Lachen I had the excuse of not knowing what was ahead. Here I was warned. I know full well that I am an idiot in not turning back. I am aware that I am repeating the idiocy that earned me a smashed ankle in Tierra del Fuego. However I remain what I was then: a brain-dead septuagenarian teenager. And turning back makes for a pathetic last hurrah. Surely to God the road must improve. I am not too far from the first hills. Reach the hills and think again…

Tar!

Narrow two-lane tar. Ah, the relief…

The road climbs towards dense pale-grey cloud. Somewhere up there is the Nechipu Pass, 1,600 metres above sea level. Creepers cascade from the swaying giants of the forest. Great leaves drip and droop from beneath the trees. Bananas compete with tree ferns, clumps of orchid on a bough, bromeliads, black rip of a landslide. The road remains mostly tar, a few potholes, rough dirt on some hairpins, but OK, manageable – and the thick rich warm scent of the cloud forest welcomes. I feel good. Continuing was the right decision. An arrow on the right side of the road advertises tea. I am travelling at less than snail's pace. Tiredness is no excuse for grabbing the handbrake. The front wheel stops dead. Over I fall. I have only the one bag and can lift the bike. I freewheel downhill to restart and punish myself by forgoing the tea.

Clouds close in. Visibility 30 feet. The road narrows. No safety parapet. Trucks loom suddenly out of dense mist. I crawl for an hour, finally stop for tea at a shack with a 4 × 4 six-seater and two trucks parked outside. The drivers crouch over a stove in the kitchen. One driver speaks a little English. 'No good,' he says of the visibility.

'No good,' I agree.

'Road no good,' he continues.

'Road no good,' I agree.

'Road bad,' he says.

'Road bad,' I repeat.

'Road very bad.'

'Very bad, yes…'

'Where you come?'

'England.'

'How old?'

'Seventy-eight.'

'Seventy-eight…' In surprise, 'Very old.' Then, 'Too old,' he says. Not encouraging…

The tea house is smaller than a double bed. I sit at the only table. A small window in the entrance door lets in a smidgen of light. Two young Tribal cops dressed in combat camouflage approach. 'Grandfather,' one calls me and leans across the table. Face close to mine, he mimes drinking. He is already drunk and armed with an automatic rifle.

'Drink,' he says.

'Tea,' I say.

His companion, also drunk, leans even closer. 'Kiss me.'

Never resist a drunk cop carrying a large gun.

I kiss both cops on the cheek.

A large-breasted woman elbows the cops aside and sets my tea on the table. One of the cops fetches a pack of sweet biscuits from the tiny shop counter. The biscuits are a present. Tea with two cops at the kissing stage of inebriation differs from my memories of tea with my grandmother – Georgian silver and bone china on a white lace tablecloth.

This is not a good day.

I crawl for a further half-hour through mostly minimal visibility. The road is narrow tar with potholes only seen at the last second. Bits of the road have fallen down the mountain. Other places boulders have fallen on the road. One light in the murk could be a bike but is more probably a truck with a faulty headlamp. Trucks keep to the centre. Fear weakens bladder control. Gloves off, dig under water-proof pants, trousers, slinky black Alpinestar long johns, underpants. Hurry. Hurry. Where is the damn thing? Ahhhhh...

Heading downhill now into a fierce bitter wind that tears small rents in the cloud. The cloud thins and lightens. Sunshine blotches the tar. The last cloud clears. A winding drop leads to a river, fol-lowed by the next climb, the road first following the river then up through thin broad-leaf to pines and rock to the Balipara Pass at 3,000 metres. Higher peaks spike the blue; sunlight flashes on cas-cade-drenched cliffs.

Balipara is one of those charmless concrete hill towns India excels at. The many army camps come of a different culture, clean, properly planned, lots of white paint, no garbage, respect for trees. See what staying 10 days with a retired colonel does to a liberal!

Cross the pass and plummet down through sparse pines to Dirang and the Hotel Pemaling where I negotiate a 50 per cent discount with the owner for a room with a superb view down the river valley. A patchwork of small fields covers the right bank and lower slopes of mountains already dark in late afternoon, peaks hidden in cloud. A kindly maid brings a Tata Sky box for the TV and the dinner menu – orders must be in by 7 p.m. Hot shower and I watch BBC World News. The receptionist brings dinner on a tray: chicken soup and vegetable momos.

'You look too tired,' he says.

Too tired to go downstairs to the dining room for dinner and I intend climbing Sela Pass in the morning.

'Will it be fine?'

'Maybe...'

Dawn and I open the curtains to the Dirang Valley, forested mountains on each side, in the far distance white peaks tinted by sunrise with a faint pink wash. Somewhere up there lies the Sela Pass. I am out of the hotel and on the road by 7 a.m. Lower Dirang has charm with balconied houses along the main street decorated with pots of primulas. Stone walls corral neat, freshly tilled fields the far side of the river. India's roads in and through and out of towns are always rough. The Sela road continues rough for a few kilometres, loose stone surface and narrowed by piles of boulders each side. Road workers squat on the boulders. Most are women, ages ranging from fresh-faced teenager to crinkle-faced grannies. Female liberation to do a man's work? Or India's standard use of women as beasts of burden?

Yes, it angers me pretty much every day of this journey. That these women respond to my *Hi* and *Good morning* is the only positive. In mainland India, wave and smile and women cover their faces against the evil eye. Or against the evil fat Old Blimp.

I expected to follow the river. The river becomes a trickle. A near vertical mountain bars the route. Water streaks mountains left and right, 500-metre falls plunging through pine forest – or 1,000-metre falls. It should be beautiful. It is beautiful. However the mountain ahead scares me. Where is the gap? A faint white line zigzags up through the pines. The many gaps in the zigs and zags must mark an absence of safety parapet. Did I write before that I don't like heights? Or, truthfully, that heights scare the shit out of me? The two Hs, Heights and Hospitals…

Even in movies, I close my eyes and shrink in the seat.

The Sela Pass is not fun. Some stretches of the road are being widened. A few short stretches have been widened. The new stretches, freshly tarred, already have deep craters. Not surprising given that the tar is less than an inch thick. Someone is making money. Lots of money. Most corners are loose rock and dirt with rain-gouged ravines on the inside of the bend. Truckers keep to the outside, which is OK if that is the driver's side of the road. Tough if it is my side. Do I go over the edge or dump myself in the ravine? At least the ravine is safe.

Parapet? Yes, in some short stretches and the mountain is near vertical. Look down and I feel sick. Worst is the wind. Come round a corner and it blasts you in the face, cold as a cold beer but minus the welcome factor. The wind comes off those snow peaks that were distant this morning and way up there. Now I am way up there with no sign of the expected gap.

I rode through deciduous forest early this morning in joyful sunshine, then tall conifers. The sun continues to shine. The trees are stunted high-altitude pine. The white peaks have become close neighbours. I stop on each corner to photograph them. Why? Mostly because photographing mountain peaks is what travellers do. I remain astride the bike while photographing. Dismounting would require trust in my legs. I stopped at an army-run café a while back. The café was a hundred yards uphill from an army camp. A sentry at the gates of the camp waved me to park on round the next corner. No cup of tea is worth walking back down to the café and then back up from the café to the bike – not at this altitude. Truth is that I am beat. The pain in my right side may be a stitch caused by holding my breath when under stress – the Sela Pass is stressful.

I've been on the road two and a half hours, uphill all the way. I've been scared much of the time. Now I've made it. I am at the top, 4,170 metres…

The pass is a narrow gap carved between two mountain peaks. My legs threaten to crumble when I dismount. A café on the left advertises tea and food. A woman serves at a small counter inside. A corridor leads to a circular space with seats and tables and with windows all the way round. I sit there a while. Nothing happens, no tea. I don't have sufficient energy to go find someone. I sit a while longer, then go back out to the bike. My legs are steadier. I lean against the café wall to steady my arms and photograph the sign-board as proof that I made it. Then I mount, press the start button and ride on down the mountain towards Tawang.

The ride down begins in sunshine with an easy stretch of

reasonable tar down a glorious upland valley, two tarns on the right, a few stunted high-altitude pines; a proper mountain burn with short, white water runs over smooth boulders into crystal pools where a worm dangled might tempt a trout. Drop a little and the road begins to zigzag, at first only a few small rhododendrons all in bud, then a couple of deep reds in bloom. Minute almost-white wild flowers speckle the turf, moss on rocks, a few tiny ferns.

Drop further and I am in yellow rhododendron territory, small and bright by the road, tree-size and pale pink through the scattered pines above sheets of drum-stick cowslip primulas the far side of the burn.

The mountain has got bored with being kind. No more gentle slopes, more a sheer drop and an end to the good road (good as in reasonable rather than good as in actually good), mostly dirt with 350-degree hairpins ripped to bits. Yaks grumble good-naturedly at being requested to move aside. Brave enough to peek over the edge and there's a village within spitting distance. Getting there takes half an hour as the road zigs and zags a half kilometre one way, half a kilometre the other and so on and so on. The first few fields are bare reddish earth. Drop further and a few green shoots grab for sunlight and white rhododendrons are in flower. Down another 300 metres and the fields are carpeted with emerald green while harvest is approaching near the valley bottom, the fall approximately 2,500 metres in 38 kilometres – the climb to the pass from Dirang was steeper.

Lunch is rice with vegetables midway down. Passengers from two eight-seater Mahindra 4x4s crowd the three tables in a tin-shack café. Two girls serve and wash plates outside at a hand pump. The girls are joyful and pretty – surely qualifications for Tribal status? I pose for cameras while waiting my turn for a seat. *Look, guys, this is me with that bearded foreign oldie and this is so-and-so sitting on the seat of the oldie's bike.* The photographing happens everywhere – and more often now than in the first weeks. People recognise me from TV and newspaper coverage. Fame? I don't believe so. More a freak status. That's OK…

The ride down from Sela has been too joyous. Punishment is inevitable. Look across the valley and a faint mist smokes the road up to Tawang, a climb of 1,600 metres in 34 kilometres through steep fields and villages. The town is shrouded in dark grey cloud. So, now, is the Sela Pass. Down in the valley an iron-girder and steel-plate bridge spans true white water. The road up is mostly rock, mud and potholes. Tires slither and bounce. The seat kicks me in the crotch. I got my second wind riding down. Second winds are temporary. Tired? Very…

Rain falls. The road has collapsed in a couple of places. Women road-workers carry baskets of aggregate on their heads. Others squat beside the road chipping boulders in the rain. Female liberation to do a man's work – or a machine's work. Children too (why aren't they at school?), armed with a heavy hammer. Their homes, shacks built of rust-decayed tin made semi-waterproof with road tar. Hill people, they grin as I pass, answer my greetings with a lifted hand and a *Hi*. My anger on their behalf won't improve their lives…

My seven-dollar Wal-Mart waterproof trousers give adequate protection against a light drizzle when strolling slowly round a municipal golf course on a warm summer's evening. I am riding a motorbike (albeit a small one) up a cold mountain in a downpour. Maybe I should be grateful that the pants act as a sieve and break some of the force of the storm – or learn to buy upmarket, say 10 or even 15 dollars. The final kilometre into Tawang is a mudslide. Tawang would look less depressing in sunshine – though not much. Tasteless concrete construction is tasteless concrete construction. Cheap paint is cheap paint. My wet Wal-Mart pants should feel right at home.

Tawang in the rain does not impress immediately as a party town, wrong vibes. A few open umbrellas scurry up the main street. Very few. A bright tartan number covers two soldiers holding hands. A good friend from Assam recommended two hotels. I choose the Tawang as the cheaper of the two. It is a modern building and should be waterproof. Two young women show me a single room at the back on the first floor designed by a specialist in B movie cellar ambience.

The women explain the temporary lack of electricity with the standard Indian apology, load shedding. I point out that a window might help. They show me a double room with twin beds and a hot-water geyser in the bathroom that will heat water once the power provider stops shedding load. The room opens off a covered walkway and on a fine day would have a fine mountain view. For now the view is black cloud, rain, parked eight-seater Mahindras and even fewer umbrellas.

I am wet and cold. There is a promise that power will return to Tawang at 7 p.m. One hour to wait and a further half-hour for the geyser to heat sufficient water for a bucket bath. The Tawang Hotel has mattresses that Indians believe to be orthopaedic and a nail-bed fakir might find comfortable. Normal mortals prefer something with more give than a concrete roadway. This roadway is liberally spread with bumps. I drag one mattress on to the other, spread the padded cotton duvet off the spare bed on top, change underwear for dry and cover myself with the second duvet and two blankets. How is it?

Cold and damp.

Power returns. I take a bucket bath and dress in everything that's dry in my rucksack. I need an umbrella. Maybe tomorrow, if the rain continues. I make a run for a Chinese restaurant three buildings down on the same street. A notice on the wall forbids smoking and alcohol. Two tables of inebriated chain-smokers provide local colour. I cross the street to a second choice, which is up an exterior circular steel staircase. My ascent is watched from the balcony by the owner. I reach the top. He says, 'Restaurant closed.'

Yes, Tawang is fun.

The last option is an archway lighted with multi-coloured bulbs down a short alley the other side of the street. Can't be the local whorehouse; whorehouses don't advertise. I hesitate. Thunder explodes followed by forked lightning. The streetlights go out. Is this a warning? But where else to go?

I make a run for the alley as a rain squall blasts up the street. A diesel generator grumbles in a shed. Double doors are heavily padded on the inside. A single candle flickers on a table. My sons might recognise the music. I have discovered Tawang's hot night spot. To be certain, I need more light. And maybe a few people. I flash my Leatherman torch round and discover a couple of plastic-covered sofas and a dozen square tables, each with four chairs and surrounding a small square dance floor. Decor is Western pop-star posters. I share the table with the candle. The candle isn't strong on conversation and I'm too tired to talk to myself. Voices come from behind a door. I tap. Then tap more firmly. Then bang. A head appears above a fake-leather bomber jacket, middle-aged with glasses.

Does he serve food?

He thinks a while before answering in the affirmative. He even switches on a light above the bar and turns a dimmer switch controlling ceiling lights from zero to .5 on a scale of zero to 10.

I order a bottle of strong Foster's (he doesn't stock normal). The beer is unique in Tawang in being warm and the chicken chow mein would satisfy a vegan in a heatwave.

Four thirty in the morning in Tawang; rain spatters the window and the room smells of wet dog. A weak bladder plus bumps in the concrete mattresses equal no sleep. A hot bucket bath might help – no electricity so return to bed and face reality. I am beat. Definitely beat. Totally beat. My back hurts. My ankle hurts. My hands hurt. Everything hurts. The Sela Pass has done for me. The road was suitable for a young, sure-footed mule – not for a septuagenarian with a fear of heights. Time has come to face reality; call a halt to exploring continents by bike; get home, invest in a ride-on lawnmower; should I crave adventure, drive three miles over the Malvern Hills of an evening and paddle in the warm waters of the outdoor pool at the Malvern Spa; for a change of climate sample the spa sauna or the steam room. In short, act my age.

Six a.m. and I search for breakfast. A newish lodging house up a side street advertises Chinese. The door is open. I order Nescafé and a plain omelette as probably safe and ask the kids running the place the cost of trucking my bike back to Assam. These are bright kids. They can spot a score. They quote 7,000 rupees as the norm – though a friend of theirs might do it for six.

I respond with one of those patronising smiles with which oldies of whatever century infuriate young whippersnappers.

The kids counter by passing off a torn patch of pale yellow art paper as an omelette and, for Nescafé, a paper cup of pale-brown lukewarm water.

I have the telephone number of a friend of a friend, Passang Tsering. An angel runs the telephone central below the Tawang Hotel. I tried calling my wife last night. The landline refused to cooperate. The angel lent me her mobile. Now she telephones Passang Tsering and gives me directions to his store a kilometre downhill in New Market.

Sunshine improves Tawang – not much but enough to make the walk enjoyable. Wild yellow primulas grow on the grass bank above the road. Tin cans planted with garden primulas splash balconies with rainbow colour. Tawang monastery up on the right dominates the route. Second largest Buddhist monastery after Lasha, it is home to 450 lamas. Have I visited? No. Will I visit? No. Monasteries and churches and temples are for prayer. Tourism strikes me as disrespectful. And the Buddhist drums in the monastery above Gangtok were a warning. Of what, I'm uncertain…

Passang Tsering runs a small store the left side of the road. A son home from college in Delhi speaks reasonable English. A younger son wears rubber gloves to hand-print Buddhist prayer flags. The father is the strong silent type. Ask him a question and he ponders deeply.

Waiting for an answer, you wonder whether he has lost the thread – or succumbed to boredom. My question is the cost of a truck to Assam.

The son has printed sufficient prayer flags for a summer solstice celebration in London's Hyde Park before Dad replies: a truck fetches fish every day from Tezpur; another fetches vegetables. Trucks travel empty of cargo south to Assam. Passenger passage is 500 rupees. Say a further 1,500 rupees for the bike.

Fish smells. Passang Tsering favours the vegetable truck. He will talk with the owner. Clouds close in as I walk back up the hill to the Tawang Hotel. Walking uphill at an altitude of 3,000 metres is moderately exhausting. I sit on a wall a while in company with a nanny goat and kid. The nanny goat is demoniacally possessed, or a close ancestor posed for medieval paintings of the devil. Wicked eyes accompany horns and a beard. Perhaps I should visit the monastery to pray for protection. A thin drizzle falls. Stupid not to have bought an umbrella…

Back at the telephone central with rain falling, I call Baby, tell her that I've crossed the Sela Pass and am safe in Tawang.

'That road was making me nervous for you,' says Baby. 'In the back of my mind I was thinking that you should stay here. So many interesting places and people you can talk to.'

I do not mention returning to Assam by truck. I glance out of the window. The road is two inches deep in hail. Bloody hell! I scuttle to the neighbouring store and buy an umbrella, then to the Chinese restaurant for a bowl of soup. Three kids enter, smoking. Apparently the NO SMOKING notice is merely for show. I cancel the soup and take my custom to the bakery.

The glass-fronted bakery counter protects trays of multi-coloured cakes and bread rolls of various shapes. The woman behind the counter is seated on a fold-up chair and is in earnest conversation on a mobile. Various customers enter the bakery, wait some time while the woman talks, leave without being served.

I sit in the bakery window seat and scribble a while in my note-book. A Suzuki jeep pulls up to the kerb. Early afternoon and daylight is minimal with cloud tails trailing between rooftops. A middle-aged man and a late-teenage girl scurry in out of the rain. The man goes directly behind the counter and stuffs rolls into brown paper bags,

20 of this, 20 of that. The teenage girl fills a plastic container with pastries before studying a tray of cupcake chemical creams. The two she finally chooses seem to me identical to the others – though I am not a specialist.

The mobile addict behind the counter stops talking on her mobile. I choose a pastry and a chocolate cake. The cake is for the angel at the telephone central.

A man, probably the mobile-addicted woman's husband, enters with a small child. He shouts at the woman. The woman shouts back. The man leaves without the child. The woman returns to her mobile. I take the cake to the angel, then return to my bedroom and climb into bed. Where else to keep warm? Maybe the power will come on in a while. Maybe not.

Thunder and the beat of heavy rain wakes me in early evening. Still no power. A single candle on the counter dimly lights the telephone central. The angel assures me that power will be restored at 7 p.m. I call the colonel in Kolkata. Where are you? Tawang. You are enjoying yourself? Not exactly.

The storm intensifies. Thunder echoes continually from mountain to mountain. Lightning lights the underneath of almost-black clouds. A massive thunderclap and steel shutters rattle shut. Tawang is closing down for Friday night. I make an umbrella-protected run for the bar/night club and order chicken kebabs. Not even a Tawang cook can produce chicken-free chicken kebabs. So where to go next? Back to bed, listen to the storm, worry that the road will fall down the mountain…

Thank the Lord for my Leatherman flashlight. What else works in Tawang – other than my bladder? I light my way to the bathroom, no power, limp back to bed, huddle under duvet and two blankets, listen to the rain, hope for more sleep.

Faint daylight seeps round the curtains. I peek down at the wet street. Nothing moves. Why would anything move? A gap in the clouds shows fresh snow on the peaks. No power so no hot water. Tawang is not my favourite place.

Six a.m. and I give up on trying to sleep. A light drizzle mists my specs as I hobble up a side street armed with my splendid new umbrella (red on red). I am due to meet Passang Tsering outside a one-burner open-front café. The loaded vegetable truck from Assam is parked across the street. A couple of landslides blocked the road yesterday for a few hours and the driver reached Tawang late. The café's cook is my informant.

How is the road now?

The cook shrugs. Heavy rain fell most of the night.

And the power supply?

A second shrug.

I sit at the only table and order tea and puris. The café is a good spot from which to watch Tawang awake. Brushing teeth out in the street is a common habit. Women with their hair uncombed scurry to the baker or collect puris from the café. The drizzle is heavier now. Bare feet in sandals slosh through puddles – so much for: *Wet feet and you'll catch your death of cold.*

Two indolent bullocks sniff at rain-melted cardboard cartons of vegetables in the back of the truck. I ought to be worried and miserable. I am content. The upright wooden chair is comfortable. Tea is hot and sweet. Puffed-up puris are fresh from the pan, dipping sauces laced with hot chilli. I can't control the weather or fix the road. Passang Tsering will negotiate the truck rate. Whatever will be will be…

Meanwhile I am doing what I enjoy most (other than eating prawns): watching people. Perhaps not all of my readers have eaten puris or know what they are. For those interested, this is the Tawang café's recipe:

2.5 cups chapati flour
2/3 cup water at room temperature
Ghee for brushing the dough
Oil for deep-frying

- Make stiff but pliable dough. Cover the dough with damp cloth and set aside for 30 minutes. Knead dough a little again. Dough should be stiff enough to roll without extra flour.
- Make small balls of the dough and cover with damp cloth.
- Take one ball of dough, dip a corner in melted ghee or oil and roll out into four- to five-inch circle.
- Repeat the process with all the balls.
- Heat plenty of oil in a kadhai until very hot.
- Drop in a puri and immediately start flicking hot oil over the top with a spatula as it puffs up into a ball. This should take only a few seconds. Flip the puri over and cook the other side until golden brown.
- Serve immediately with dipping sauces or curries.

Tawang is a study in genetic diversity. The angel of the telephone central is Tawang Mompa. Typical of her community, she is slight of build, fine-featured. Mountain Mompa are squatter and speak a different language unintelligible to the city folk. Valley Mompa speak a third language, equally foreign to mountain and city folk. Cross the pass to the next valley and you find a fourth language and a fifth and a sixth. Division by language enfeebles Arunachal as a political unit. Buddhism is the sole unifier.

Passang Tsering's great-grandparents were immigrants from Lhasa and the family's home language remains Tibetan. At six foot, he is taller than the Mompa, powerfully built, his features born of the Himalayan steppes. His mountaineer's stride is scornful of the slope up from the main street. He wears a puffa jacket over a tartan shirt, jeans and work boots. He shakes and folds a khaki-green umbrella before entering the café.

I have met with much kindness and generosity on this journey. Passang Tsering is my latest benefactor. I watch from inside the café as he negotiates with the truck owner and the driver. The driver is young, perhaps foolhardy. Angel told me yesterday that two couples in a saloon car went over the edge on the Sela Pass the day I crossed. They were killed and this is a common occurrence. The retired Customs officer on the road to Puri warned that truck drivers took pills to keep awake at the wheel (presumably speed). The army commander asked whether I had seen an Indian truck driver wearing spectacles. No, not that I've noticed. The implication is obvious.

Does Tawang have an oculist? Should I ask Passang Tsering to have the young driver's eyesight tested? Or should I close my own eyes as we cross the Sela Pass? If we cross the Sela Pass. A Mahindra that left Tawang before dawn this morning has returned to report the road closed by a landslide. The road may reopen by mid-afternoon, meanwhile rain falls steadily from black clouds and Passang Tsering warns that the chances of leaving today are slim.

The army commander expects me for dinner at his camp tomorrow and I intend taking the sleeper train from Guwahati to Delhi at the end of the week.

Or am I condemned to a life sentence in Tawang?

Is Tawang Purgatory?

Or Hell?

Or would sunshine transform the town?

Even electricity would help, light, hot water.

A decision has been taken. We will load the bike early tomorrow and drive straight through to Assam. I accost a blond foreign couple mooching up the main street in the rain. Are they Czechs?

How did I guess?

We three are the only Europeans in town and two Czechs are on my permit for Arunachal.

The Czechs paid 8,000 rupees for the permit.

I paid 5,000 rupees. A total of 13,000.

A Mr Wanga arranged the permit. He initially demanded 9,000 from the Czechs. He claimed to be an influential politician and would obtain the permit within 48 hours once they had transferred the fee. They waited six days.

The male Czech is tall with dreadlocks and loathes India. All Indians are on the make. Everyone has tried to rip him off.

I have enjoyed extraordinary hospitality, though telling him is wasted effort. His English is too limited and he speaks neither French nor Spanish – nor Russian. Surely Russian was obligatory at school? He dislikes Russians (understandable in a Czech) and never learned.

She is better educated and marginally less negative. We shelter in a mini restaurant on the main street. The owner, a woman, is seated behind a cash box. She ignores us. Perhaps she is related to the mobile-phone addict at the bakery. Or suffers from poor eyesight. Or dislikes foreigners…

Half an hour of difficult conversation passes before a girl appears from the kitchen. I order soup. The Czechs drink water.

What to do in Tawang on an electricity-deprived rain-drenched afternoon under low dark clouds? Not a lot. Daylight is insufficient in my room for reading. I take my book to the smoke-free Chinese restaurant. Two of the six tables are occupied by inebriated chain-smokers. University students sit at a third. I ask why there is no electricity.

The transformer is damaged.

I repeat the question.

They repeat the answer.

I say, 'Wrong answer. There is no electricity because there is no spare transformer and there is no spare transformer because you don't shout. Do any of you vote?'

None of them. There's no point. Nothing changes.

To which I say, 'Nothing will change if you don't vote. Or, at least, shout. Go shout outside the electricity company's office.'

I have made them uncomfortable. I am uncomfortable. Tawang is too wet and too cold for an instant revolution. Better go sit in the corner at the telephone central, talk with the angel and call Baby.

I tell Baby that I will truck the bike back to Assam.

'I didn't want to tell you with all these experienced travellers

giving you advice,' says Baby. 'In the back of my mind I was thinking that you should stay here. So many things to see. The farm and
my cousin's house on the hill.'

'Watch cricket in comfort on a large-screen TV,' I say.

'That's what I'm telling you,' says Baby. 'Look where all this adven-
turing has got you. You are not a young man.'

True...

Two young drunks loll against the counter at the telephone central.
One drunk drops the chip from his mobile. Both drunks bend to
pick it up. Their heads collide and they shout at each other. The
angel solves whatever problem they have.

I remark to the angel that drunkenness seems common in Tawang.

'They fight when they get drunk,' she says. 'They go home and
hit their wives.'

'Always?'

'Always.'

Will she marry?

Not in Tawang. An elder brother emigrated to Canada. Angel is
waiting for a visa.

Tawang is awaking reluctantly to one more wet, grey, chilly day and
no electricity. The driver, an assistant and a small boy are lashing the
Honda down in the back of the pick-up. Perhaps I should be helping
– or directing. The seat beside the stove in the café gives a good view.
Tea is hot, puris crisp, dipping sauce deliciously fiery.

Departure is at hand; driver and self enjoy heated comfort in the
cab while the boy shelters under a black garbage bag in the back.
Landslips are being cleared on the outskirts of town. Gas stations
are closed – no electricity for the pumps. Roadside stores are possible sources of petrol and the driver stops frequently. The boy is the
handbrake, leaping out to slam a wooden block under the onside rear
tyre. We are fortunate twice, 20 litres each time, sufficient to get us
to the frontier. Down to the first valley and up the other side is stop

and start. Terraces have collapsed on to the road; work gangs are ill equipped. Fresh snow whitens the peaks either side of the Sela Pass. Once through the pass and we are on solider ground. The driver speeds up. He is a curly-haired kid, early twenties, and ruled by a streak of sadism. My nervousness at the speed excites him. I order him to slow down. He responds by accelerating and weaving on the straight stretches: Yves Montand driving the truck in the 1953 thriller, *The Wages of Fear*. Yves Montand goes over the edge...

And the driver is merely softening me up. The fee agreed with Passang Tsering is inadequate. He wants double. I will agree to anything just so he slows down. What did you expect? Courage?

Poor visibility in the cloud forest slows him, and the cab of a heavy Mahindra pick-up is more protective than the saddle of a 125. I feel braver – less afraid. The mud follows. Six days of rain have turned it from tough going for a bike into impossible. We pass an abandoned scooter and overtake two locals pushing their bikes. The driver won't stop for fear of getting stuck. Dusk has fallen. We reach the frontier, papers checked and the driver demanding the doubled payment to unload the bike.

I am at his mercy and act meek. 'Please drive me on a couple of kilometres to the Eco Camp track...'

We have gone half the distance. An army Suzuki jeep approaches. A powerful spotlight shines into the cab, followed by a roar of, 'Simon...'

Special Forces surround the pick-up. The driver trembles as the commanding officer directs his soldiers to unload the Honda. Always the gentleman (or the fool), I pay the originally agreed fee and tip the juvenile two-legged handbrake.

Dinner under canvas in the army camp is both pleasurable and enlightening. The major and his second-in-command sit one side of the trestle table. I sit the other. A civilian in the camp is against regulations. A foreign civilian (almost certainly a spy) is a court martial offence. The second-in-command is a senior warrant officer with nearly 20 years of service. He is both cautious and protective of the major. My presence makes him uncomfortable. So does the beer. The major is talking of things best left unmentioned. Corruption is his chief target, yes, even in the army that was once clean of sin. He is confronted by it here on a daily basis, arresting illegal loggers in the National Park. The judge releases them and they are back the next week. Frustrated, the major now acts as judge and jailer. The logger is given a smacking (the major's word), and left for the night tied to the tree in the centre of the camp – an involuntary tree hugger. Released in the morning, he will warn fellow loggers of the new regime. Stealing truckloads of boulders from the river is the major's second concern. Boulders slow the river's flow. Removing them causes further erosion of the riverbanks. The major found a convoy of six trucks parked by the river while I was in Tawang. No purpose served in arresting the drivers. Drivers were merely hired hands. The truck owners are never punished – until this occasion when, enraged, the major shredded every wheel on the trucks with his sub-machine gun. The trucks remain in situ. No wonder his second-in-command seems anxious and excuses himself – early parade in the morning.

The major opens two more bottles – these are the big ones.

At partition his family lost their farm in what is now Pakistan Punjab. His father is a truck driver. In rank the major has reached the glass ceiling for truck driver's sons. He plans to take early retirement, join one of the private armies operating in Iraq, Blackwater, etc. The major is newly married, has a baby son. Two years in Iraq and he will be able to buy a farm.

If an IED doesn't blow him to kingdom come.

He shrugs at the risk.

Well past midnight and time for old men to be in bed. A driver together with a two-man escort transports me to the Eco Camp. The escorts take an arm each. These are big men. I march as deliberately upright as an English gentleman should. My feet are some distance clear of the ground.

The major's driver fetches me from the Eco Camp in the morning. Two fried eggs seated on a slab of mutton should be welcome. I don't feel my best. The sun is unnecessarily bright and I have a final 200 kilometres to ride. This is not a day for adventure either in mutton or on roads. I take the highway through the town of Tezpur and cross the Brahmaputra by the Kolia Bhomora Setu Bridge; three kilometres of stressed concrete and no shade seems endless in my delicate state. Finally the run to Guwahati on what I think of as the Kaziranga highway and my motorcycle journey is done, 16,000 kilometres of plain and mountain and the baby Honda never hesitated.

I am safe in my room at Baby's and having an early night. Baby said that I looked worn.

'The road,' I said. 'Even in the pick-up…'

'That's what I was telling you,' said Baby.

We are lunching tomorrow at the dosa restaurant and the banker and his wife who were at Wild Grass have asked me to dinner. The following day, my last in Assam, there is a party at a businessman's home. Meanwhile I must reserve my train ticket to Delhi together with the paperwork for the bike; check at the station's cargo desk that packing material is available. The Rajdhani Express is the fastest train. It departs at seven in the morning and arrives in Delhi at 10.15 the following day. Baby advises an air-conditioned, two-tier sleeper rather than first class. The difference in cost is 80 per cent.

Dinner with the banker and his family is little different from dinner in London – perhaps slightly more cultured in conversation, the early-teenage daughters certainly more courteous.

The following night's party brings disaster. India's rapidly expanding economy has given birth to a new commercial class – not super rich but successful local business people: tailored jeans, two cars in the garage, air conditioning, kids away at private school, holidays abroad. The house is new, modern, big windows. Living room is on the first floor with views across a lushly tropical garden, pool terrace, caned loungers. Space is ample for the 40 or so guests, relations mostly, three generations. I have dressed in dark blue trousers together with a loose shirt of thin homespun in lighter blue, no undershirt so no braces. Baby approves: 'Very smart, Simon…'

Midway through the evening and I am seated in a deep armchair, a second whisky sour in one hand, side plate of lamb samosas in the other. A dowager of importance arrives. I am introduced. How to rise with full hands and no side table for glass or plate? Stomach muscles tighten, paunch withdraws. Chill air as the trousers slip. No way to halt the dreaded descent. The dowager relieves me of glass and plate. I bow before her, hands pawing for trouser waistband.

'Don't worry, Simon,' calls my host's mother from the far side of the room. 'At your age, you don't have much left to hide.'

So falls the final vestige of a once all-powerful Empire.

The bike was wrapped with straw and hessian yesterday at the station. A cab is ordered for 6:15. Baby in white pyjamas sits with me at the dining table. Baby's and her brother's generosity have eased these last weeks. Baby has given me both a home and an insight into an influential stratum of Assam society. Her kindness was the antidote to my trials in Arunachal Pradesh. The cab comes. The couple who care for Baby load my bags. Baby and I face each other. A quick hug. More and I might cry. Tiredness does that to a man and I am tired. I've been away six months. I need to be back in Herefordshire with Bernadette, share experiences with my sons, exchange cuddles with my grandchildren, finally relax.

The train leaves on time. I share a four-berth compartment in an air-conditioned carriage with one man. The air conditioning doesn't work. The conductor assures us that it will work. The man with whom I share the compartment speaks basic English. He is a diesel engineer and travels on this train once or twice a month. He has minimal faith in the air conditioning being repaired.

The conductor is a believer. At Patna, he assures us.

Patna is the capital of Bihar.

Of all states, Bihar is reputed to be the poorest and most corrupt. The chief minister, a woman, succeeded her husband when he was jailed for embezzlement. Forty years have passed since I drove through Bihar. I recall hour after hour of wet dirt roads behind long trains of ox carts. I was with a family friend from England, Sarah Duke. We were driving from Kathmandu to Pokhara; this in the years before the east-west road in Nepal had been built. We pulled in at a government guest house one night. The string on the string beds had rotted. So had the mosquito nets. We tried sleeping on the dining table. Mosquitoes devoured us. An hour after midnight and we gave up, repacked the car and continued the drive only to be stopped a half-day short of Pokhara by a river in full spate. The river ran in a narrow ravine. A footbridge connected the two banks and a road bridge was under construction to replace a chain raft that carried two cars but wasn't operational with the river this high. The steel skeleton of the road bridge projected midway across the ravine and was supported by a temporary pillar. The builders had built a cofferdam of sandbags round the pillar. The river was rising and they had run out of sandbags. Two of the workers were waving joss sticks at the water while chanting prayers. Sarah crossed by the footbridge and got a lift on to Pokhara. I waited two nights at the road camp for the river to drop sufficiently for the chain raft. The cook at the road camp had ambitions to develop the pure sand chapati. And, yes, the supporting pillar did fall

The train isn't as bad as the road camp – though we were four hours late in reaching Delhi and the air conditioning was never fixed. Unloading the bike takes a further hour. I have been invited by a young couple, ex-marines, I met at Wild Grass to stay at their home in the US Embassy compound. My hosts have finished their Delhi posting, China next stop. Personal possessions are already boxed. Their neighbours have real American T-bones on the barbecue, cold beer by the case. Americans abroad are always so immediately welcoming.

Delhi is hot. *The Times of India* reports a politician's bodyguard dead of heat exhaustion while waiting by the car. Monday I fly to Mumbai. Sunday morning is an invitation to a breakfast ride with a Delhi biker club. The leader will be outside the US Embassy compound at 5 a.m. I must be up at 4:30.

The compound is in New Delhi – new as in designed for the public servants of the British Raj. Streets are wide and tree-lined, bungalows in shaded gardens. Security is tight at the compound. Surrounding walls are high, guard post at the solid steel gates. I wheel the Honda out and wait. From the end of the street comes the powerful burble of a 2300 cc Triumph Rocket. Lift the Triumph on to its stand and I would have difficulty keeping up.

Second to arrive is a gleaming BMW R1200. I am not what the riders expected. They are not what I expected.

A rapid decision is reached: the BMW will rendezvous with the rest of their gang; the Triumph will take me home for breakfast. He is a graphic artist with his own ad agency and in the final stages of a bitter divorce. The wife gets their home out in one of Delhi's older garden suburbs. The about-to-be ex believes that good taste is pale cream. The Triumph has been painting vividly vengeful murals across the walls – comic book heroes, zigzag lightning, ceiling-high exclamation marks. The Triumph's new love is in residence and his father is visiting – a dear man, gently academic. The new love is an old love from high school on the run from an arranged marriage to a husband who beat her up. Breakfast is croissants and coffee. Honda will send a rider to collect my bike in the morning. So ends my motorcycle experience of India.

I fly home tomorrow. I am at the Taj, Mumbai. I have a room in the new tower block with a view of the bay. The room is modern five-star luxury. It isn't the Taj. Nor is the dining room. That once-great room is dressed for a sales conference. Noticeboards diminish its size; chandeliers have lost their glory; the almost religious hush is non-existent. I mourn the waiters silent on thick carpet, fresh flowers on every table, polished silver, tablecloths and napkins of a starched cotton seemingly too heavy to be disturbed by the strongest gale.

There was never need for more than one restaurant. No sane person would have eaten elsewhere. Now there are a plethora: Grill room, Golden Dragon, Souk, Shamiana, Wasabi by Morimoto and so on.

My guide to the hotel's desecration is the head of public relations. She is intelligent, young and beautiful, a woman of graceful movements. We play with a luncheon salad, a single glass of chilled white.

I try and fail to imagine Darab Tata, Caroline facing him at a centre table, Darab duty-bound by friendship with Caroline's father to persuade Caroline to end her guru obsession. Caroline stubborn from head to the tip of her saffron-painted toes.

I say nothing. My loss is private.

The internet has banished privacy. Records are computerised, a tap on the keyboard and our secrets are revealed. This young woman is adept at unearthing connections.

'You were a friend of Mr Darab Tata's,' she remarks.

'Yes,' I say.

Long pause, then, somewhat embarrassed, 'How did you meet Mr Tata?'

An even longer pause, 'Weren't you a sort of hippy in those days?'

I picture myself following the maître d'hotel to Darab's table, starched white homespun, shoulder-length curls, beads. So, yes, in a way, but never convinced or convincing. A fortnight in Goa was a surfeit of the marijuana routine, the tissue-paper profundities. For this I could have remained in Ibiza. India was for exploration. Bombay was concerts of classical music. Some we attended were by private invitation to a rich man's salon. Vanessa and I were fortunate in our introductions.

Deidre is in Mumbai. We dine together on minuscule and monstrously expensive artworks of Japanese cuisine. I have parked a bottle of Sauvignon Blanc in the mini fridge in my room. We sit on the balcony, moonlight, wine, the bay spread below us, small boats at anchor.

This is not a prelude to attempted seduction.

In my extreme youth I would have been boringly insistent only to be foiled by the elasticated barricades of corsets and suspender belts. Followed were the years in which I believed that not making the effort was demeaning to the recipient, impolite. Now respect has caught up with me – and age rather than wisdom. I have only to look in the mirror...

Nor is this a time for conversation. We have had our separate experience of the subcontinent – time to reflect. And, for me, to remember. Out beyond the boats lies the island of Elephanta, a jagged shadow against the sea. I recall the cave temple within the island, standing in front of the great mask of Shiva. Being drawn into Shiva's eyes, drawn in and held somewhere other. Vanessa was with me. She spoke to me. I didn't hear. Shiva shuttered his eyes. I was released. Vanessa asked later what had happened. I told her. She thought me brave in talking of it. I am not brave.

I turn to Deidre. Her arms are bare, her skin holds a golden sheen.

'You're crying.'

'Not really,' I say.

I escort her to the door. 'I've so enjoyed your company,' is the truth. 'You've been very kind.'

Her lips brush my cheek.

'Do please get your doctorate and let's keep in touch,' I add.

The door closes on what I should have said: that I'm not a good person. I've done a lot of harm in my life, hurt badly those who trusted me. Betrayed all my relationships, wives, children, by running away and only to look for comfort elsewhere. When all's said and done, that's what travelling so often is: running away from the responsibilities of adult life, moving on before your frailties are discovered.

Confiteor omnipotens Deus...

Acknowledgements

Many people have helped over the months of this journey with friendship, hospitality and advice. This Indian odyssey is as much theirs as mine. My special thanks go to Fiona and Paul, Colonel Rajen Bali, the quartet of my fellow adventurers in Sikkim and to the Royal Gentleman, his sister and brother-in-law; to Baby and her brother, to Noel and Deidre; to the Taj Hotel Group, particularly the staff and management at the Usha Kiran Palace whose cosseting cured me of bronchitis, Mrs Modhurima Sinha in Kolkata and the kindly Romanian butler at the Prime Minister's suite in the London Taj; to Honda India for supplying the 125 cc Stunner and always to my brother, Antony, whose support makes my journeys possible. Finally, my sincere apologies to the dowager for losing my trousers.